NASCAR
50 GREATEST DRIVERS

Six of NASCAR's 50 Greatest Drivers ran "nose to tail" through the turns of the road course at Northern California's Sears Point Raceway on May 4, 1997. In order were race winner Mark Martin, Terry Labonte, Rusty Wallace, Jeff Gordon, Dale Jarrett, and Bill Elliott.

NASCAR
50 GREATEST DRIVERS

BY BILL CENTER & BOB MOORE

HarperHorizon

An imprint of HarperCollins*Publishers*

A TEHABI BOOK

NASCAR would like to give special thanks to the panel of judges for their time and effort in choosing NASCAR's 50 Greatest Drivers

50 GREATEST DRIVERS PANEL OF JUDGES
Bobby Allison
Jack Arute
Buck Baker
Richard Childress
John Cooper
Dick Dolan
Junie Donleavy
Dale Earnhardt
Chris Economacki
Bill Elliott
Joe Epton
Tim Flock
Jim Foster
Ray Fox
Jeff Gordon
Barney Hall
Bob Harmon
Eloise Hawkins
Rick Hendrick
Tom Higgins
Phil Holmer
Jim Hunter
Jack Ingram
Ned Jarrett
Junior Johnson
Terry Labonte
Fred Lorenzen
Hershel McGriff
Ralph Moody
Bud Moore
Cotton Owens
Earl Parker Sr.
Raymond Parks
Benny Parsons
David Pearson
Lee Petty
Richard Petty
Benny Phillips
Larry Phillips
Les Richter
T. Wayne Robertson
Paul Sawyer
Ken Squier
Herb Thomas
Steve Waid
Rusty Wallace
Darrell Waltrip
Waddell Wilson
Glen Wood
Leonard Wood
Cale Yarborough
Robert Yates

Tehabi Books, which designed and produced *NASCAR 50 Greatest Drivers*, has conceived and produced many award-winning, visually oriented books. "Tehabi," which symbolizes the spirit of teamwork, derives its name from the Hopi Indian tribe of the southwestern United States. Tehabi Books is located in Del Mar, California.
Chris Capen—*President*; Tom Lewis—*Editorial and Design Director*; Sharon Lewis—*Controller*; Andy Lewis—*Art Director*; Nancy Cash—*Managing Editor*; Sam Lewis—*Webmaster*; Ross Eberman—*Director of Corporate Sales*; Tim Connolly—*Sales and Marketing Manager*; Sarah Morgans—*Copy Editor*; Gail Fink—*Copy Proofer*.

www.tehabi.com

NASCAR 50 Greatest Drivers was published by HarperHorizon,
an Imprint of HarperCollins Publishers Inc., 10 East 53rd Street, New York, NY 10022.
John Silbersack—*Senior Vice President and Publishing Director*;
Ken Fund—*Senior Vice President Finance and Operations*;
Frank Fochetta—*Vice President and Director of HarperCollins Enterprises*;
Patricia Teberg—*Director of Brand Publishing*; Amy Wasserman—*Marketing Director*;
Lois Brown—*Senior Editor*; Jeannette Jacobs—*Assoc. Art Director*.

www.harpercollins.com

With special thanks to key individuals at NASCAR for their contributions in the creation of *NASCAR 50 Greatest Drivers*.
Paul Brooks—*Director of Special Projects and Publishing*;
Kelly Crouch—*Editorial Manager*; Kevin Triplett—*Director of Operations*.

www.nascar.com

Photography credits appear on page 112.

Library of Congress Cataloging-in-Publication Data

Center, Bill.
    NASCAR 50 Greatest Drivers / by Bill Center & Bob Moore.
        p.   cm.
    "A Tehabi book."
    ISBN: 0-06-107330-X (softcover).
    1. Automobile racing drivers—United States. 2. Automobile racing drivers—Rating of—United States—Juvenile literature.
3. NASCAR (Association) I. Moore, Bob, 1940- . II. Title. III. Title: 50 greatest drivers. IV. Title NASCAR fifty greatest drivers.
GV1032.A1C45   1998
796.72′092′2
[B]—DC21   98-12421
                                                          CIP

98 99 00 01 02 / TB 10 9 8 7 6 5 4 3 2 1

This edition is printed on acid-free paper that meets the American National Standards Institute Z39.48 Standard.

Printed in Korea through Dai Nippon Printing Co., Ltd.

Martinsville Speedway was still a dirt track when Bob Welborn (49) led the pack through a turn on May 3, 1959.
Welborn drove a Chevrolet to back-to-back wins at Martinsville in 1957 and 1958.

It takes cunning and nerve—grit and determination combined with expert driving skills and superb coordination—to carry NASCAR drivers and their machines across the finish line.

For fifty years NASCAR drivers have pushed themselves and their cars to the limit and beyond, always meeting the challenge of change head-on. NASCAR drivers have gone from racing boxy sedans on vintage, rutted-dirt-and-sand courses to running today's sleek racing hybrids on high-banked super-speedways, constantly adjusting, inventing, and remodeling themselves and their cars to go the distance and stay the course.

"One reason why we didn't have more five-hundred-mile races back then is because the cars and drivers wouldn't last five hundred miles on a lot of the tracks we ran," pioneering legend Herb Thomas once remarked. "We, and I mean the car and driver, took a beating."

Despite the advancements in technology and funding, the constant has been the men behind the wheel. But a few of them have stood out from the rest. Fifty drivers have contributed more to the sport through their victories, innovations, and the personal mark they have put on NASCAR racing. Some drivers had long and storied careers. Others had brief but spectacular ones. All are legends.

As part of its 50th anniversary celebration, NASCAR (National Association of Stock Car Auto Racing) polled a group of fifty-two experts—drivers, team owners, crew chiefs, track operators, writers, and broadcasters—to select fifty drivers whose achievements both span and epitomize NASCAR's first half-century of accomplishment and growth.

The panel selected a cross section of drivers that represents every era of NASCAR's advancement as well as every racing division. These eras mark the unbroken lineage of NASCAR's very best.

NASCAR's **Pioneers** took their back-roads experience onto the first primitive racetracks, joining with NASCAR founder Bill France Sr. to create honest and reliable sanctioned races.

the Heroes

The greats from those earliest races were Buck Baker, Red Byron, Tim Flock, Junior Johnson, Lee Petty, Marshall Teague, Herb Thomas, Curtis Turner, Bob Welborn, and Rex White.

The Challengers made the leap onto the first superspeedways, finessing their skills to keep up with modernization. This second era began with the opening of the high-banked, 2.5-mile tri-oval at Daytona International Speedway. They were Ralph Earnhardt, Ned Jarrett, Fred Lorenzen, Tiny Lund, Cotton Owens, Marvin Panch, Fireball Roberts, Joe Weatherly, Glen Wood, and LeeRoy Yarbrough.

By the mid 60s, the high-speed ovals and hotter cars attracted more national interest in NASCAR. But it was **The Giants,** whose personalities came to match the power of their cars, who developed a fan loyalty not experienced until that time. The spotlight fell on Bobby Allison, Buddy Baker, Jerry Cook, Richie Evans, Red Farmer, Ray Hendrick, Bobby Isaac, Richard Petty, David Pearson, and Cale Yarborough.

The New Generation brought NASCAR into homes across the land via television and developed a new class of champions who were as sharp before the camera and microphone as they were behind the wheel.

A whole new wave of fans discovered NASCAR through Geoff Bodine, Neil Bonnett, A.J. Foyt, Harry Gant, Jack Ingram, Alan Kulwicki, Hershel McGriff, Benny Parsons, Tim Richmond, and Darrell Waltrip.

The Future Legends, who will take NASCAR into the next century, have already begun to carve out their place in racing history with the great runs of Dale Earnhardt, Bill Elliott, Ernie Irvan, Terry Labonte, Mark Martin, Rusty Wallace, and the tenacious owner-driver efforts of Ricky Rudd. Second-generation heirs Davey Allison and Dale Jarrett carried the legacy forward at the start of the '90s. And Jeff Gordon has already won two NASCAR Winston Cup Series championships.

Fifty years, however, hasn't altered the one fact—great drivers are great drivers—no matter what era they raced in.

"These are the drivers who made and make NASCAR fans stand on their feet and cheer," said NASCAR President Bill France Jr., as he announced this elite group. "These are the drivers who made NASCAR history."

Curtis Turner (26) leads Ford teammate Joe Weatherly (12) through the north turn of Daytona's famed Beach-Road course during a 1956 race.

The Pettys, son Richard (43) and father Lee (42), have their Plymouths side by side on the front row for a race at the legendary Bowman-Gray Stadium in Winston-Salem, North Carolina.

Start at the beginning—even before that.

"Before NASCAR, there was chaos," pioneer car owner Raymond Parks recalled. "Nobody knew who to trust. Stock car racing was a crazy business."

That changed over four days in December of 1947 during a meeting led by Bill France Sr. at the Streamline Hotel in Daytona Beach, Florida.

The National Association for Stock Car Auto Racing was formed to promote and regulate the sport of stock car racing.

"It's hard to look back now and see where we came from, even with NASCAR," says Herb Thomas, NASCAR's first two-time champion.

"Most all our tracks were dirt. Some were pretty good. But others were mud bowls in the winter and spring and rutted hard as rock in the summer. And no one I knew was a full-time racer at the start. We drove trucks and worked as mechanics. But the racin' was still racin'."

The first race sanctioned by NASCAR was a modified race on Daytona's famed Beach-Road course on February 15, 1948. A crowd estimated at 14,000 saw Robert "Red" Byron finish fifteen seconds ahead of hometown hero Marshall Teague to claim NASCAR's first checkered flag.

NASCAR sanctioned fifty-two races that year. Byron won eleven and claimed the organization's first championship in the Modified Division. But it wasn't until 1949 that France's dream was truly unveiled.

France believed NASCAR's future was in fans watching drivers race the same cars they could drive on streets and highways rather than modified and souped-up older coupes.

And in 1949, he introduced the Strictly Stock class as NASCAR's premier division. The first race of the new class was on

June 19, 1949, on the three-quarter-mile Charlotte Speedway. France didn't have to wait long to have the Strictly Stock fundamental challenged. North Carolina's Glenn Dunnaway finished three laps ahead of the nearest competition. But Dunnaway was disqualified for having modified springs in the rear end of his 1947 Ford. Jim Roper, who had driven his Lincoln from Great Bend, Kansas, after reading about the race in a comic strip, was declared the winner.

Byron won two of 1949's Strictly Stock races and won that series' first season championship. His award: $5,800.

But NASCAR was up and running.

The premier series was renamed the NASCAR Grand National Division in 1950 (later to become the NASCAR Winston Cup Series). The schedule was expanded to nineteen races in 1950 and forty-one in 1951. In addition to the Grand National and Modified Divisions, NASCAR added a Short Track Division in 1951 and a Speedway Division for Indy-type cars in 1952.

Drivers started flocking to NASCAR, including a family of drivers named Flock—brothers Tim, Fonty, and Bob, and sister Ethel.

"Racing was different back then," said Tim Flock. "If you had enough in your pockets, you could race three and four nights a week. When the money ran out, you'd go home until you could save up enough to fix the car. But if you got to the track, you could always find someone to help you get ready."

Drivers were rugged in those days. So were the cars. Both had to be because the tracks delivered beatings.

Thomas favored the Hudson Hornet not because it was necessarily faster than the opposition, but because the cars were built like tanks. En route to his two titles, Thomas "saw a lot of fast cars shake to pieces during races."

But there was steady advancement through the '50s. As the tracks improved, the more powerful and faster cars took control. In 1955–56, the Chrysler 300s of team magnate Carl Kiekhaefer won fifty-two of ninety races and two championships. The sport was already changing.

Rex White didn't fit the mold of NASCAR's early champions.

He was only 5' 4" tall and often had trouble reaching the pedals of the Chevrolets he drove. He was quiet.

And instead of running whiskey across rural roads as a youth, White honed his driving skills delivering eggs for farmers around Taylorsville, North Carolina.

"I learned to drive carefully and consistently," White said.

And those attributes paid dividends during a nine-year NASCAR Winston Cup career that saw him win the title in 1960 and finish in the top ten six times. Also, White twice finished second in NASCAR's Late Model Short Track Division final standings in the late 1950s.

While other drivers finished with the checkered flag or a heap of broken parts, White succeeded by being consistent. He finished in the top five in 110 of his 233 career starts and ran outside of the top ten only 30 percent of the time.

"White was a real good short-track racer. That was his specialty," said Cotton Owens. "He was a master at driving the short tracks."

White's success was closely linked to crew chief Louis Clements. Although their Chevrolets lacked the power to compete on the superspeedways, Clements and White became masters at setting their cars up for the shorter ovals that dominated the NASCAR schedule at the time.

Injured in a nonracing accident after the Pan-American Road Race in 1964, White returned briefly in the NASCAR Sportsman Division in 1965 before retiring.

Rex White

"Rex was real smooth. Smooth and patient. When you were racing Rex for the win, you couldn't relax until the checkered flag fell. He was very tenacious."

—NED JARRETT

Born: August 17, 1929
Hometown: Spartanburg, South Carolina
The File: White won the 1960 NASCAR Winston Cup title in his fifth season on the tour. Won 12 percent (28) of his career 233 starts, which ranks him among the top dozen in winning percentage. Finished in the top ten in six of the nine years he competed on NASCAR's premier tour. Only one of White's victories, the 1962 Dixie 400 at Atlanta, came on a superspeedway.

"Buck could drive and race any car they ever built. He was one of the most versatile drivers I've ever seen. And he was fast in everything."
—BENNY PARSONS

Born: March 4, 1919
Hometown: Charlotte, North Carolina
The File: Baker became the first driver to win consecutive NASCAR Winston Cup titles in 1956–57. His first championship came while driving a Chrysler for car owner Carl Kiekhaefer. The second came in a Chevrolet as an owner-driver. Twenty-four of his 46 career wins and 17 of his 44 career poles came during his two championship seasons. Ranks eleventh in career wins, ninth in poles, and seventh in starts (631). Also was the first champion of NASCAR's IndyCar-like Speedway Division in 1952.

Buck Baker

Elzie Wylie "Buck" Baker was driving a city bus in his hometown of Charlotte, North Carolina, when he decided to try his hand at racing in 1939.

"I was scared to death the first time I got out on that track," Baker recalled. "I can't remember when I couldn't drive a car, but this was different."

By the time he was finished, Baker's diversified career spanned four decades. He ran modifieds as well as NASCAR Winston machines and open-wheel cars. His last race was the 1976 Firecracker 400.

"I always thought I'd go until I saw there were other guys who could do the job better," said Baker, who was fifty-seven at the time of his last race.

Baker's earliest NASCAR success came in modifieds. He won 10 straight races in 1950 and 12 of 14 during one stretch of the 1951 season. In 1952, Baker was the first champion of the NASCAR Speedway Division for Indy-type cars. In addition to back-to-back NASCAR Winston Cup titles in 1956–57, Baker finished second in points twice and was among the top five in the final standings nine times. After he stopped running full time in the NASCAR Winston Cup Series in 1967, Baker competed in the NASCAR Grand American Division and had 8 wins and 44 top-five finishes in 109 starts.

"Buck was real aggressive. He was one of those guys who didn't like running second or third," said Cotton Owens. "He was going to the front."

When he finally retired from driving, Buck Baker opened a driving school that became the first stop for a number of newcomers.

Born: March 12, 1915 (d. 1960)
Hometown: Anniston, Alabama
The File: Robert "Red" Byron won NASCAR's first sanctioned race in 1948 and the first two NASCAR season championships Took NASCAR's first checkered flag in a Modified race on Daytona's famed Beach-Road course on February 15, 1948, averaging 75.94 miles per hour (mph). First championship was in the Modified class in 1948. The next year he stepped up to NASCAR's Strictly Stock class an won the first of what would eventually become the NASCAR Winston Cup Championship. Competed only one more season in NASCAR.

"Red really knew cars. In a lot of ways, I thought he was before his time."

—CAR OWNER RAYMOND PARKS

Red Byron

On the surface, Red Byron seemed a simple man. A tail gunner on a bomber during World War II, Byron returned home to open a garage near Atlanta, Georgia, at a time when Atlanta was the hub of stock car racing.

Many of the hot cars of the day doubled at night as whiskey runners. Byron, however, built cars strictly for racing and became one of the earliest and more influential drivers to support Bill France Sr.'s formation of NASCAR in 1947.

Byron supported NASCAR on and off the track. In 1947, when the featured division was Modifieds, Byron captured both NASCAR's first race and its first season championship in a spirited duel with Fonty Flock.

A year later, France decided that his new Strictly Stock Division would become NASCAR's hallmark class. Byron favored the Modified class, but decided to back France in whichever direction France wanted to go. It was a pivotal decision. Byron had emerged as NASCAR's most popular driver.

Byron won two races in 1949 and NASCAR's first Strictly Stock championship with an Oldsmobile Rocket 88. But his interests were changing.

Byron dreamed of building a sports car for the 24 Hours of Le Mans. He had always been intrigued by road racing and became one of America's leading road-racing advocates. At the time of his death in 1960, Byron was trying to design and build a purely American sports car.

"Red was a very smart man and a very good driver who could have won a lot more races if he had stuck around longer," said Herb Thomas.

"I remember the monkey. Sometimes, Tim would get you laughing and you'd forget everything else and he'd be concentrating on the race." —HERB THOMAS

Born: May 11, 1924 (d. 1998)
Hometown: Ft. Payne, Alabama
The File: A true NASCAR pioneer, Flock finished fifth in the inaugural NASCAR championship race on June 19, 1949, at Charlotte Speedway. Won the NASCAR Winston Cup title in 1952 and 1955. His 18 victories (in 45 races) in 1955 stood as a record until Richard Petty won 27 races in 1967. Flock's 19 poles in 1955 still stand as a record. His winning percentage of 21.2 (40 wins in 189 starts) is the highest in NASCAR Winston Cup history. Finished in the top five in 55 percent of his starts. Won NASCAR's only sports car race in 1955 driving a Mercedes-Benz 300 SL Gullwing. Great racing family included brothers Bob and Fonty and sister Ethel.

Tim Flock

He was the son of a daredevil and sometimes drove with a monkey as his copilot. But make no mistake about Tim Flock. The NASCAR pioneer was one of the sport's greatest drivers.

"I always thought you could do both: win and have fun," Flock once said, while describing his style. "It was a lesson the kids learned from my dad."

"Dad" was Carl Lee Flock, a tightrope walker whose adventuresome nature was handed down to his three sons and daughter.

During the early 1950s, Tim, Bob, and Fonty Flock were joined in a race by sister Ethel Flock Mobley, marking the only time in NASCAR Winston Cup history that four siblings competed in the same race.

"The three of us boys had trouble and Ethel finished ahead of us," recalled Tim. "The teasing got so bad for a couple of weeks that we had to go into hiding."

Tim Flock raced eight times with his pet monkey, "Jocko Flocko," in the co-pilot seat. But the monkey broke free during a 1953 race at Raleigh, North Carolina, and grabbed Tim by the neck, holding on for dear life. Flock had to make an extra pit stop to de-monkey his car, which ended up costing him the race.

Buck Baker recalls: "Tim had fun. He was a character and I mean that in a very nice way. But when he turned it on, he was as tough as there was to beat."

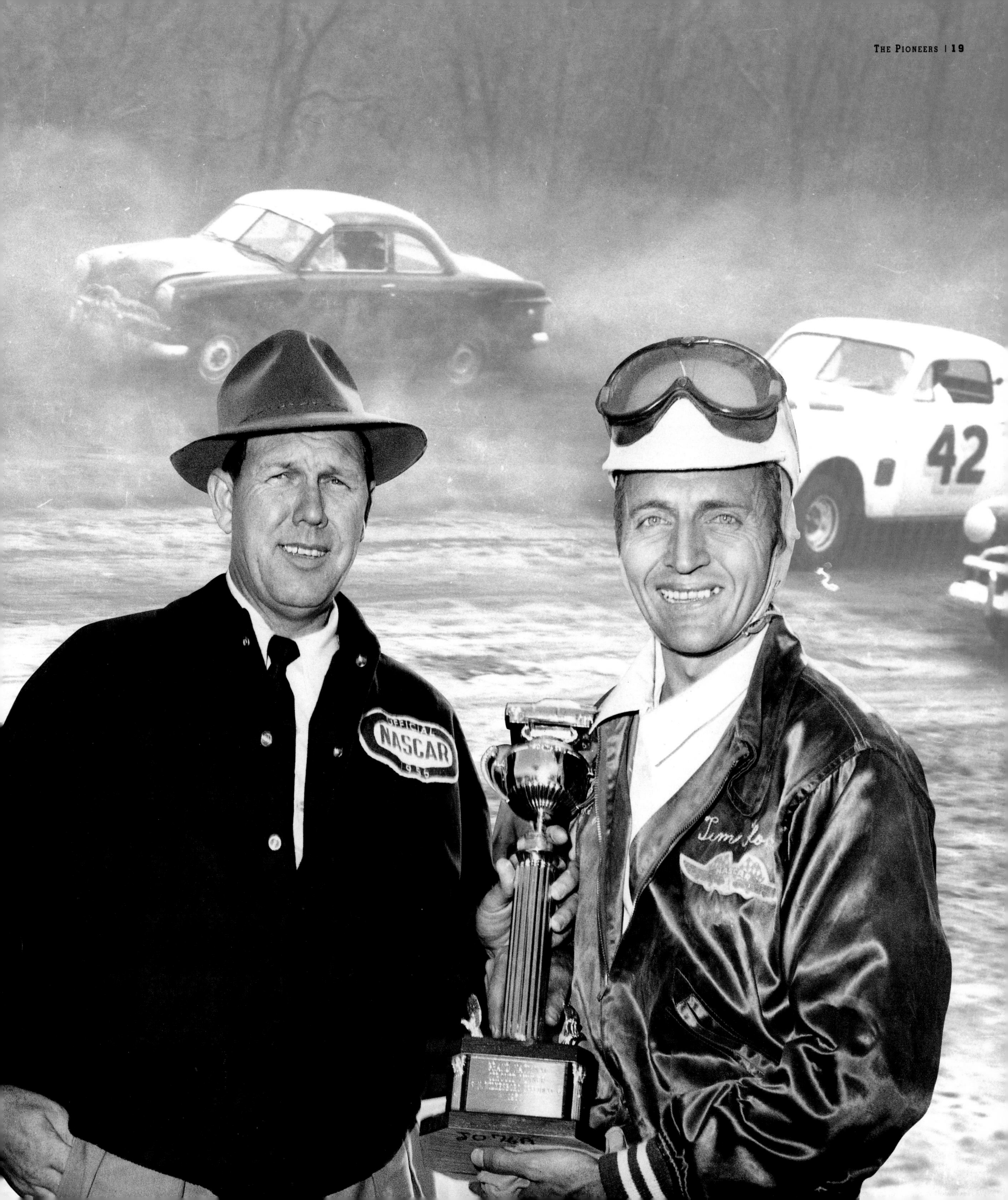
OFFICIAL
NASCAR
42

Born: June 28, 1931
Hometown: Ronda, North Carolina
The File: Johnson's career went from running moonshine on North Carolina's back roads to winning races on the track to becoming one of the most successful owners on the NASCAR Winston Cup tour. On the track, Johnson won 50 NASCAR Winston Cup races but never finished higher than sixth in the points. Won 13 of 36 starts in 1965. Very aggressive driver who also ranks eighth with 47 poles. Retired as a driver in 1966 and became a car owner. Thirty-eight drivers won a total of 119 races for Johnson. Cale Yarborough and Darrell Waltrip each won 3 NASCAR Winston Cup titles in Johnson cars. Johnson was also instrumental in linking NASCAR with title sponsor R. J. Reynolds.

"Junior would go as hard as he could as long as he could. He would never, ever slow up no matter how far he was ahead. If the car didn't break or crash, you couldn't catch him." —TIM FLOCK

Junior Johnson

Robert Glenn Johnson Jr. got his start running whiskey on the back roads of North Carolina.

And he was proud of it.

"Moonshiners put more time, energy, thought, and love into their cars than any racers ever will," Johnson once said. "Lose on the track and you go home. Lose with a load of whiskey and you go to jail."

Johnson was a one-of-a-kind person who eventually changed the sport without ever forgetting his roots. He loved that he could do more with a 1940 Ford powered by a supercharged 454-cubic-inch Cadillac engine than he could do on the track.

"Rules hamper innovation," he once said through a wry smile. "It'd be more fun if they just let us see what we could do. Call it e*ngin*uity."

Still, he lived inside NASCAR's rules and became its first folk hero thanks partly to Thomas Wolfe's classic essay, "The Last American Hero." Junior Johnson was the prototypical NASCAR Winston Cup driver: committed, shrewd, daring, and down-home.

"Junior was a pure driver," Richard Petty said years ago. As a driver, Johnson retired young at the age of thirty-five. He says he lost his love for going in circles. "I always favored racing on those back roads through the mountains," he would say later. And he said he found more pleasure in building cars.

His motto:

"Win, wreck, or blow."

He used to take those little ol' Plymouths and just outthink and outlast people."

Lee Petty is best known these days as the patriarch of the most famous family in racing. Son Richard is "the King" of NASCAR Winston Cup racing. Grandson Kyle is among the more popular drivers on the tour.

Lee was quite a driver in his own right. And he was there from day one.

Before Bill France Sr. formed NASCAR, Petty, a mechanic by trade, spent his spare hours drag racing down backcountry roads near the Petty home. He pocketed some extra cash by winning bets on his ability as a driver . . . and as a mechanic.

Petty entered NASCAR's first race at Charlotte in June of 1949. He drove a '46 Buick to the race (which doubled as the family car)—then drove it in the race. Midway through the event, he rolled the machine.

"Some of my best memories were driving to races with my dad," said Richard. "He loved cars . . ."

Petty spent much of his career beating back the opposition with underpowered Plymouths. Petty's forte was finding a way to get his cars to the finish in those early days of rutted dirt tracks and purely stock cars. He was NASCAR Winston Cup's all-time race winner until his son, Richard took over the spot in 1964.

As NASCAR grew, the elder Petty also became instrumental in developing safer cars.

Tim Flock said: "Lee was into all of racing. He understood the car as well as driving. He knew you didn't have to always be the fastest to be first."

Lee Petty

Born: March 14, 1914
Hometown: Level Cross, North Carolina
The File: When he retired as a driver, Petty was the only three-time NASCAR Winston Cup champion and the all-time leader with 54 race wins. Still ranks seventh on the all-time list of winners. Won the inaugural Daytona 500 at Daytona International Speedway in 1959 in a photo finish with Johnny Beauchamp that took three days to decide. Ranked in the top five in the final standings in 11 of his 16 full seasons. Dubbed "Mr. Consistency" by rivals, Petty finished in the top ten of 32 of the 34 races he started in 1954 en route to his first title.

Marshall Teague

Marshall Teague knew dirt and engines. He knew how to make a car work in the dirt—which was crucial to success in NASCAR's formative years.

But to say Marshall Teague was only a great dirt-track racer would not do justice to a man who became one of racing's most versatile drivers.

Teague raced in the Indy 500 (he finished seventh in 1957) and the Pan-American Road Race as well as NASCAR and other stock car events.

His story, however, is linked closely to NASCAR's roots at Daytona Beach, Florida, and the Beach-Road course. Teague grew up in Daytona Beach and routinely drove on the beach sands. So it is no surprise that Teague would later become known as "the King of the Beach" for his prowess on running on the tricky oceanfront course.

Teague also prepared some of NASCAR's faster cars in his Daytona Beach garage during those early years. The Hudson Motor Company brought Teague and Herb Thomas together as a team. The big, slab-sided, six-cylinder Hudsons became known as Teaguemobiles. While Thomas was winning two NASCAR championships in the Hudson, Teague was winning two AAA titles while dividing his time between the two series.

Born: February 17, 1922 (d. 1959)
Hometown: Daytona Beach, Florida
The File: Teague was known as "the King of the Beach" for his successes on Daytona's famed 4.7-mile Beach-Road course. After winning the 200-mile Modified race on the beach at Daytona in 1949, Teague scored two of his seven NASCAR Winston Cup victories on the Beach-Road course. Teague trailed Red Byron by 15 seconds to finish second in NASCAR's first race February 15, 1948. Scored five of his seven career wins in 1951.

"Marshall was really good on dirt. I liked his style so much that I kind of copied my driving style after his. He was real smooth."

—COTTON OWENS

"Bob dominated the Convertible Division the way Richard Petty did the Winston Cup ten to fifteen years later." —NED JARRETT

Born: May 5, 1928 (d. 1997)
Hometown: Denton, North Carolina
The File: Welborn began his racing career in the NASCAR Modified Division at Bowman-Gray Stadium in Winston-Salem, North Carolina. Moved up to the NASCAR Winston Cup Series in 1953 and finished fourth in the 1955 point standings. Won 9 races and claimed 7 poles in 183 NASCAR Winston Cup starts. But it was in NASCAR's Convertible Class that Welborn made his mark, winning the championship three straight seasons (1956–58) before NASCAR discontinued the series. At one time, he held 20 qualifying and race records.

N.C.   BOB WELBORN   49

TRADERS CHEVROLET
COMPANY

Gra
PISTON

Bob Welborn

Richard Petty is "the King."

Bob Welborn was "the King of Convertibles."

And had superspeedways not come along, Welborn might just have been NASCAR's winningest driver. His only problem was a slight miscalculation.

Welborn was off to a successful start in the NASCAR Winston Cup Series—although he didn't win his first race until 1957, he finished fourth in the final points in 1955—when he misread NASCAR's intentions.

He thought NASCAR's new Convertible class would become the sport's premier division because the spectators could see the drivers in the open cockpits. So he switched to convertibles and won three straight series titles (1956–58).

But the opening of Daytona International Speedway in 1959 spelled doom for the convertibles. The superspeedways demanded better aerodynamics and the convertibles were buffeted by cockpit turbulence.

Welborn returned to the NASCAR Winston Cup Series, where he won 9 races in 183 starts. But he retired from racing in 1964, thinking NASCAR had peaked. Again, he was wrong.

Still, Welborn scored some notable achievements. He won the first race ever at Daytona International Speedway, averaging 143.198 mph to win a one-hundred-mile qualifier before the inaugural Daytona 500 in 1959. He won a second one-hundred-mile qualifying race in 1960. He had twenty-six victories in convertibles in addition to his nine NASCAR Winston Cup wins.

Outwardly shy and unassuming, Herb Thomas was driving trucks and delivering goods across the coastal plain and sand-hill sections of North Carolina when Bill France Sr. organized NASCAR.

"In the back of my mind, I always wanted to race cars because I thought I was a pretty good driver," Thomas said. "NASCAR gave me the opportunity."

Herb Thomas

And Herb Thomas, one of NASCAR's true pioneers, ran with that opportunity.

Thomas was the first two-time champion in what was to become the premier NASCAR Winston Cup Series. He was the first driver to win multiple races on NASCAR's first superspeedway, Darlington Raceway.

Early in his career, Thomas won with Hudson Hornets that he owned and prepared. Later he drove for Carl Kiekhaefer.

"I liked the Hudson because it was big and sturdy and rugged," said Thomas. "There were a lot of dirt tracks back then. And some weren't in real good shape. The Hudson just kept running and running."

His cars were much like Thomas. Rugged. And they just kept running. Several bad accidents in the late 1950s cut short Thomas's racing career.

"Herb was rugged and dependable. He was very strong," said, Tim Flock. "In those early days, the cars would beat you up in a long race. But Herb was so tough that it didn't bother him at all."

But he never stopped driving. He founded his own trucking company in 1962 and spent another two decades on the road.

"He had to be good to win forty-eight races in only six years. From a winning standpoint, Herb was as fierce a competitor as anybody." —RICHARD PETTY

Born: April 6, 1923
Hometown: Sanford, North Carolina
The File: A truck driver by trade, Thomas was one of NASCAR's pioneers and became the first two-time champion of NASCAR's premier series in 1951 and 1953. Driving a sturdy Hudson Hornet for most of his career, he won 48 races and claimed 39 poles in 230 starts. Almost four decades after he retired, he still ranked tenth among the all-time NASCAR Winston Cup race winners. First three-time winner of the Southern 500 at Darlington in 1951, 1954, and 1955.

Curtis Turner

Curtis Turner loved to race.

Curtis Turner loved life.

And the flamboyant Virginian pursued both his loves to the fullest during a multifaceted life. It was Turner who said: "Run it till it breaks, or wins."

"Curtis never did anything half way," said Junior Johnson. "He threw himself a hundred percent into everything."

Many rivals considered Turner the greatest driver ever on dirt. His skills may have been the result of clandestine runs in his youth on backcountry roads, but Turner was equally at home on asphalt.

His all-or-nothing approach to racing created some memorable battles. His aggressive duels with Joe Weatherly in NASCAR's Convertible Division produced some of the sport's top races in the 1950s. In 1961, Turner came out second-best to teammate Fred Lorenzen in a fender-smashing run to the checkered flag at the Rebel 300 at Darlington.

And in 1965, after being away from NASCAR for four seasons, Turner returned to beat Cale Yarborough in the first race at Rockingham, North Carolina.

Turner was equally successful away from the track. A businessman who specialized in lumber and real estate, Turner helped create Charlotte Motor Speedway.

Born: April 12, 1924 (d. 1970)
Hometown: Roanoke, Virginia
The File: Called the "Blond Blizzard," Turner was a fun-loving, bigger-than-life figure. Credited with 17 NASCAR Winston Cup victories, but probably won more than 350 NASCAR and other stock car events during his career. Won the fourth race of the inaugural NASCAR Winston Cup season in 1949. In 1950, led the series in laps completed (1,626), laps led (1,110), and races led (12). Built Charlotte Motor Speedway.

"Curtis Turner was the greatest race driver I have ever seen."

—BILL FRANCE SR.

In a duel between two of NASCAR 50 Greatest Drivers, Marvin Panch (98) moves to the inside of Tiny Lund (47) during the 1958 race on Daytona's Beach-Road course.

The late '50s and early '60s were a time of tremendous change for NASCAR.

Dirt tracks gave way to paved ovals and eventually the superspeedways that would become NASCAR's signature circuits.

The cars became more aerodynamic. The Oldsmobile Rocket 88s and boxy Hudson Hornets driven by the earliest pioneer champions were replaced by the more powerful Chrysler 300s of the mid 50s and again by the fastback Fords, Plymouths, and Dodges of the early '60s.

As the speeds increased, the drivers were forced to adjust their skills and craft new techniques. Glenn "Fireball" Roberts was the first to discover the art of drafting in another car's wake and to employ the strategy of the slingshot pass.

Again, it was Bill France Sr. at the forefront of this period of rapid expansion. The revolution started when he opened the Daytona International Speedway in 1959.

But the cornerstone was laid in 1950 in an old peanut farm at a crossroads near the tiny South Carolina town of Darlington.

Enamored by a visit to the Indianapolis 500, Harold Brasington decided to build a speedway in the South for stock cars, which until that point had run shorter distances on shorter ovals.

Brasington built a high-banked, egg-shaped oval track that originally measured 1.25 miles that was both unique and enduring. To this day, Darlington Raceway hosts one of NASCAR's premier events.

Darlington pointed NASCAR in a new direction. When it opened in 1950, Darlington Raceway was home to the NASCAR's first five-hundred-mile race. It would remain NASCAR's only superspeedway for almost a decade. Then came a period of growth that reshaped NASCAR.

the Challengers

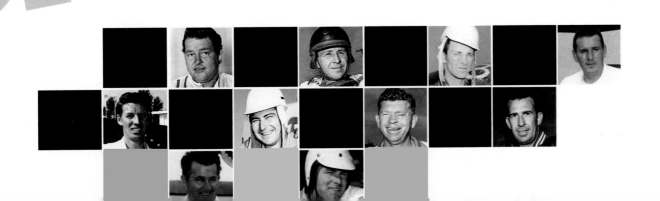

It began with the Daytona International Speedway, NASCAR's most cherished shrine.

There had been racing on Daytona's famed Beach-Road course since 1902. But for NASCAR to prosper and expand, the sport needed larger facilities that could both host larger crowds and capture the public's imagination.

Daytona wowed them. It was the same 2.5-mile length as Indy with a couple twists that would become NASCAR trademarks: high-banked turns (31 degrees at Daytona) and a tri-oval shape that brought fans closer to the action and forced drivers to retool their methods.

"It was also a time of adjustment for the drivers," said Lee Petty, who won that inaugural Daytona 500 in 1959. "None of us were used to going that fast."

But NASCAR had switched gears into high speed.

The 1.5-mile Charlotte Motor Speedway opened in 1960. So did the 1.522-mile oval at Atlanta Motor Speedway. The 1-mile North Carolina Motor Speedway opened in 1965. The 2-mile, D-shaped Michigan International Speedway opened in 1969. Later that same year, France's second diamond, Talladega Superspeedway—the longest (2.66 miles) and fastest superspeedway in the NASCAR family—opened in eastern Alabama.

While at that time the shorter ovals were also being modernized, it was the brilliance of the new facilities and the thrill of the higher speeds that began to attract national attention to what had been a mostly southern sport.

Safety improvements to the cars also had to keep pace with the burgeoning speeds. Full roll cages, rubber fuel cells, and new tires reduced the fear of high-speed blowouts.

"So much was happening so fast that at times it was hard to keep up with the changes," said former-driver-turned-TV-commentator Ned Jarrett. "But it was exciting because we knew the sport was taking off."

Drivers like Roberts, Joe Weatherly, and Jarrett became national figures. Fred Lorenzen, driving for the powerful Holman-Moody team, became the first driver to hit six figures when he won $122,588 in 1963.

"The sport shot ahead," said Lorenzen.

DeWayne "Tiny" Lund will be forever remembered in NASCAR for the events of 1963 at the Daytona 500. During a practice session for a sports car test—a Maserrati—Lund helped to save the life of Marvin Panch, pulling the driver from a burning car at considerable risk to his own life. Lund was awarded a Carnegie Medal for his heroism.

Panch and the Wood Brothers team found another way to reward Lund. They put Lund in the Ford that Panch was supposed to drive in the Daytona 500. To complete one of NASCAR's finest stories, Lund won the Daytona 500. That was one of only two races Lund won in a twenty-one-year career that saw him start 303 NASCAR Winston Cup races. As a racer, Lund was better known for his success on short tracks in the sporty Grand American Division. He won four NASCAR titles in Grand American cars (1968, 1970, 1971, and 1973). The 6-foot-5, 270-pound Lund was anything but Tiny. He once said his passions in life were "racing, eating, and fishing and not particularly in that order." He owned a fishing camp on Lake Moultrie, South Carolina, and at one time held the world record for freshwater striped bass.

Early in his racing career, Lund favored the open-wheel sprint and modified cars but was too big to climb into the cockpit.

Tiny Lund

> "Tiny was a determined driver and the strongest, quickest, big guy you've ever seen."
>
> —CAR OWNER LEONARD WOOD

Born: March 3, 1936 (d. 1975)
Hometown: Cross, South Carolina
The File: A native of Iowa who starred in football and basketball in high school, Lund had a first love of racing and he moved south after serving in the air force to pursue his dream. Most of Lund's early success came in NASCAR Sportsman races on the Carolinas circuit. Won the 1963 Daytona 500 and later became a four-time champion in the NASCAR Grand American class. Late in his career, Lund raced in Japan as an ambassador for NASCAR.

16

"*Roberts was before his time. He had the talent and flair to get the publicity. He was the first real superstar the sport had. And he had as much to do with making the sport what it is today as anyone else.*" —NED JARRETT

Glenn "Fireball" Roberts

Alas, the greatest nickname in racing had nothing to do with cars. Glenn Roberts was dubbed "Fireball" for the fastball he threw in high school and later at the University of Florida, where he studied mechanical engineering.

But the "Fireball" was perfect for Roberts' driving style.

Handsome, daring, intelligent, and sharp with the post-race quotes, Roberts became NASCAR's first superstar—a personality whose lure extended well beyond the sport's traditional southern base. Fireball's popularity helped NASCAR's recognition expand during the move from the dirt tracks to the superspeedways, where he became one of the sport's first high-speed champions.

He was far more than popular, however. Fireball Roberts was respected by his peers for his knowledge, ability, and daring. He was one of the first drivers to understand the concept of drafting and the slingshot pass.

"Fireball was a man first, a competitor second, and a teacher third. I saw him take young guys aside many times and tell them something that would help," said Richard Petty. "I guess he helped the sport more than anybody."

Roberts knew the dynamics of cars and engines. He also knew the dynamics of spectator sports.

Born: January 20, 1929 (d. 1964)
Hometown: Daytona Beach, Florida
The File: Arguably the greatest driver never to win a NASCAR Winston Cup title. Roberts had 32 wins in his NASCAR Winston Cup career, including 4 at both Daytona International Speedway and Darlington Raceway. Considered the early king of superspeedways. Finished second in points as a rookie in 1950. In 1958, raced only 10 times but had 6 wins, a second, and a third. In 1959, Roberts' Pontiac started 46 in the Daytona 500, but was leading after 23 laps only to be sidelined by a midrace fuel pump failure. His death from pneumonia and complications from injuries six weeks after an accident in the 1964 World 600 at Charlotte led to safety improvements in the sport.

Cotton Owens

The son of a garage owner, Everett Owens never wandered far from his roots.

Nicknamed "Cotton" for his white hair, Owens grew up with a love of racing. And although he became a talented driver, he started and concluded his career in the pits.

"Cotton was one of us in the sport who loved racing more than winning," said car owner Junie Donlavey.

Owens' first opportunity in the sport came when powerful car-owner Gober Sosebee offered Cotton a job as a mechanic on a modified.

"When I was in the navy during World War II, I thought a lot about getting home and seeing the races again," Owens once recalled. "Sosebee offered me a job in racing. That was as good as it could get."

It wasn't. A year later, in 1947, Sosebee offered Owens a chance to drive. And Cotton quickly became one of the first stars of NASCAR's Modified Division.

After winning more than 200 Modified races, including 24 straight, Owens decided to move up to the NASCAR Winston Cup Series. He would start 160 races and win 9 at the premier level. But he would find most of his success in that division as a car owner and mechanic.

In 1963, Owens ran a stable of five cars on the NASCAR Winston Cup Series and in 1966 he was the crew chief of the Dodge that David Pearson drove to his first title.

> "He's as nice a man as you'd ever want to meet. Anyone who ever had a question could find an answer and a pat on the back over in Cotton's garage."
>
> —DAVID PEARSON

Born: May 21, 1924
Hometown: Spartanburg, South Carolina
The File: Owens began his career in the NASCAR Modified Division, where he won more than 200 races. Fifty-four of his wins came during the 1950–51 seasons, including a run of 24 straight. Although he finished seventh in the inaugural Southern 500 in 1950, Owens didn't start running regularly in the NASCAR Winston Cup Series until 1957. Won at least one NASCAR Winston Cup race annually between 1957 and 1962. Finished with 9 career wins in 160 starts.

"*He was my hero. Always has been, always will be. To this day, I still use things he taught me. In my opinion, he was the greatest. What I have I owe in large part to him. And what I have I would give up today to have him back.*" —Dale Earnhardt

Born: February 29, 1928 (d. 1973)
Hometown: Kannapolis, North Carolina
The File: The patriarch of the Earnhardt racing family was an excellent short-track driver. Won more than 250 short-track races during his career. Won NASCAR's Sportsman Division championship in 1956. Made only 51 NASCAR Winston Cup starts during his career. In 1961, he posted seven top-ten finishes in eight starts and finished 17th in the NASCAR Winston Cup standings.

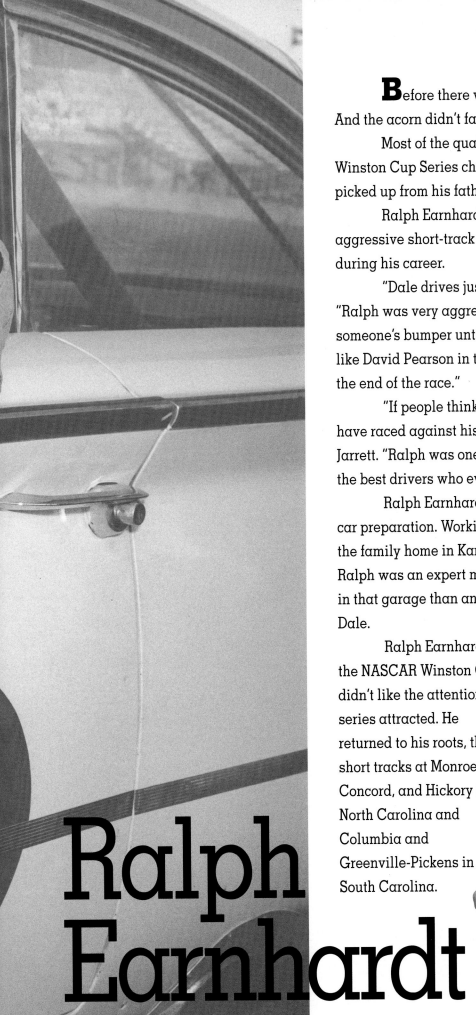

Before there was Dale Earnhardt, there was father Ralph. And the acorn didn't fall very far from the giant oak.

Most of the qualities that made seven-time NASCAR Winston Cup Series champion Dale Earnhardt a great driver were picked up from his father.

Ralph Earnhardt was a tough, hardheaded, and extremely aggressive short-track champion who won more than 250 races during his career.

"Dale drives just like his daddy," said driver Cotton Owens. "Ralph was very aggressive, but very smart. He liked to sit on someone's bumper until the very end and then go for it. Ralph was like David Pearson in that regard. He never showed his hand until the end of the race."

"If people think Dale is tough, they should have raced against his daddy," said driver Ned Jarrett. "Ralph was one tough racer. He was one of the best drivers who ever sat behind the wheel."

Ralph Earnhardt was also meticulous at car preparation. Working in his garage behind the family home in Kannapolis, North Carolina, Ralph was an expert mechanic. "I learned more in that garage than anywhere else," recalled Dale.

Ralph Earnhardt tried his hand briefly at the NASCAR Winston Cup tour. But he didn't like the attention the series attracted. He returned to his roots, the short tracks at Monroe, Concord, and Hickory in North Carolina and Columbia and Greenville-Pickens in South Carolina.

Ralph Earnhardt

> *"Nobody knew anything about Marvin until he showed up and started racing. Then we learned he was pretty good."*
> —FRED LORENZEN

Marvin Panch didn't start out to be a driver. In high school, he dreamed of playing football and baseball. And his first endeavor in professional sports was as a boxer. Even when his work in a Northern California garage sparked an interest in cars, Panch saw his racing future as an owner and mechanic of jalopies. That changed one night when his driver failed to show. Marvin drove the car and won.

"Why pay someone else to win when, if I win, I keep all the money," Panch reasoned in the pragmatic style that would mark his career. Panch always thought things out.

After winning the California NASCAR Late Model crown in 1950 and 1951, Panch entered the army for two years. When his tour was over, he consolidated his business interests and moved to Charlotte, North Carolina, in time to compete in the 1957 NASCAR Winston Cup season. He caught everyone by surprise. As a totally unknown rookie, Panch won six races and had twenty-seven top-ten finishes to finish second in points to defending champ Buck Baker. Panch used his winnings to buy a farm near Daytona Beach, Florida.

As a driver, Panch was branching out. He ran only eight NASCAR Winston Cup races in 1962, but finished five times in the top five. He was also running sports cars.

Marvin Panch

Born: May 28, 1926
Hometown: Oakland, California
The File: Marvin was the first product of West Coast racing to campaign successfully on the NASCAR Winston Cup tour. Won 17 of 216 career NASCAR Winston Cup starts. Most notable victory was the 1961 Daytona 500 in a Pontiac for Smokey Yunick's team. Best season was 1957 when he won 6 races and had 27 top-ten finishes in 42 starts and finished second to Buck Baker in the standings.

"He was really good, and very smooth on asphalt. You have to be smooth to keep from burning your tires."

—CREW CHIEF
LEONARD WOOD

Glen Wood

The Wood Brothers are synonymous in NASCAR circles for total preparation and excellent pit work.

But before Glen and Leonard formed a behind-the-scenes team, Glen took his own turn behind the wheel.

It started innocently enough. Wood and some friends bought a modified in 1950 to run on dirt tracks. "It was just for fun," Wood recalled. "We wanted to see what we could do with a car. But we didn't have the money to hire a driver."

So Glen was nominated to fill the position. And he filled it well.

But his interests were always more focused on preparing the car than racing it. "I loved the driving," he said. "But it was always an area where I thought we could hire better people than me. As for preparing and servicing the car, we did pretty well."

So well that in 1965, Jimmy Clark asked the Wood Brothers to man his pits in the Indy 500—a rare honor for a NASCAR Winston Cup crew in those days. The Wood Brothers turned out the best pit stops at the Indy 500, helping Clark to win the race.

The Wood Brothers became the superstars of pit row. Their drivers read like a Who's Who: David Pearson, Cale Yarborough, A.J. Foyt, Parnelli Jones, Dan Gurney, Buddy Baker, Dale Jarrett, Neil Bonnett.

Glen Wood was an excellent driver, but he once changed an alternator in thirty-five seconds. You can find a lot of good drivers. Find another person who can change an alternator in thirty-five seconds.

Born: July 18, 1925
Hometown: Stuart, Virginia
The File: Although he became better known as half of the famed Wood Brothers team, Glen was quite a driver. Won NASCAR's North Carolina Sportsman title in 1954. Three years later, he placed third in NASCAR's Convertible Division. Two years later, was elected NASCAR's Most Popular Driver. Won 3 races and claimed 4 poles in just 9 races in 1960. Won 4 races in 62 career NASCAR Winston Cup starts.

"As great a driver as he was—and he was great—he's done far more for this sport in the television booth than most of us ever did on the track." —RICHARD PETTY

Ned Jarrett

When Ned Jarrett retired in 1966 it seemed like NASCAR was suffering a huge loss.

Jarrett was only thirty-five. He had already won two NASCAR Winston Cup Series championships and fifty races. He was emerging as one of the sport's superstars.

But he wanted to spend more time with his young family and "pursue other interests."

NASCAR should be grateful Jarrett retired when he did. One of those "other interests" turned out to be television and Jarrett has become one of the reasons why NASCAR blossomed on the tube in the last two decades.

Jarrett's sharp, witty analysis and behind-the-scenes look at NASCAR drivers and the sport has helped win over millions of new fans and has enriched the races for NASCAR's loyal partisans.

"I want the viewers to see the drivers as people and develop an understanding of the racer's love of the sport," Jarrett said. Like most of his comments, it was right on the mark.

Not bad for a man who started his driving career under an assumed name (John Lentz) at Hickory Motor Speedway near his North Carolina home.

Jarrett's father had frowned on Ned becoming a racer. But the ruse ended quickly when Jarrett won one of his first starts.

"Son, if you're going to drive, you might as well get credit for it," reasoned Homer Jarrett.

Ned Jarrett has been getting and giving credit ever since.

"Ned's one of NASCAR's leading ambassadors," said Bill Elliott.

Born: October 12, 1932
Hometown: Newton, North Carolina
The File: "Gentleman Ned" won the NASCAR Winston Cup title in 1961 and 1965. One of nine drivers with 50 or more career wins in NASCAR's top series. Won 14 percent of his career starts and finished in the top five of 53 percent of starts. Prior to winning his two NASCAR Winston Cup titles, won two NASCAR Busch Series championships in 1957 and 1958. Most memorable victory was winning the 1965 Southern 500 at Darlington by 14 laps.

"I always thought he quit in his prime. Had Fred continued to race, he might have been high on the all-time list." —RICHARD PETTY

Looking back, Fred Lorenzen wished he hadn't stopped racing so early in life. "And I wished I had raced more often than I did," he said.

When he did race, Lorenzen, whose Illinois base was far from NASCAR's southern roots, was among the toughest drivers to beat on the track.

His 26 NASCAR Winston Cup wins came in just 158 starts. He also claimed 33 poles and 75 top-five finishes.

Lorenzen won 16 percent of his starts and finished in the top five 47 percent of the time. Those percentages are close to the best in the sport.

But he never ran a complete season.

In 1963, Lorenzen finished third in points and became the first driver to top $100,000 in single-season earnings. He won 6 races and had 21 top-five finishes in 29 starts. But the season numbered 54 races.

A year later, Lorenzen won 8 of the 16 races he started. But he missed 45 races.

Lorenzen was thirty-two years old when he retired for the first time in 1967. After a three-year hiatus, he raced 29 times between 1970 and 1982 before retiring for keeps at the age of forty-one.

"I just woke up one day and that was it," he explained of his early retirement. "Looking back, it was a stupid thing to do. I got out of it too soon."

Born: December 30, 1934
Hometown: Elmhurst, Illinois
The File: "Fast Freddie" may be best known for being the first driver to win more than $100,000 in a single season when he pocketed $122,588 in 1963. Finished second in the Daytona 500 that year and won the race two years later. Equally adept at winning on short tracks and superspeedways. In 1964, he won 8 of the 16 races he entered and finished thirteenth in NASCAR Winston Cup points despite not entering 45 of the season's sixty-one races. Won races in seven of the twelve years he raced on the NASCAR Winston Cup tour and his 26 wins represented a 16 percent success rate.

Fred Lorenzen

Joe Weatherly

Fun-loving. Mischievous. Daredevil. Racer. Champion.

All those words—and more—can be used to describe Joe Weatherly.

"Little Joe" liked to have a good time. He was the ultimate practical joker—a man who deserved his title as the "Clown Prince of Stock Car Racing."

But when Weatherly was on the track, he was all business. He didn't like to lose—and he didn't lose very often in a career that began on motorcycles and culminated with wins in three NASCAR divisions from Modifieds to the NASCAR Winston Cup Series.

Weatherly's contribution to NASCAR and racing goes far beyond wins, however. His charismatic personality made him popular with the fans and he became one of NASCAR's first superstars. He helped attract a number of new fans to the sport and went out of his way to promote NASCAR through numerous media engagements.

He was also a master of coining catchy phrases that helped describe racing. Weatherly is best known for his description of his style as "flat-out and belly-to-the-ground."

Weatherly's twenty-five NASCAR Winston Cup wins came in a short, four-year period. He died in an accident in Riverside, California, in 1964.

"Joe was one of the pioneers in helping to develop automobile racing. . . . Plus, he was one great racer."
—Track owner Paul Sawyer

Born: May 29, 1922 (d. 1964)
Hometown: Norfolk, Virginia
The File: One of NASCAR's earliest superstars, Weatherly was also a very versatile racer. Won 3 American Motorcyclist Association championships between 1946 and 1950. Turned to car racing in 1951 in NASCAR's Modified Division. Won 101 races in the 1952 and 1953 seasons and claimed the 1953 NASCAR Modified Division championship. From 1956 through 1959, Weatherly was one of the top drivers in NASCAR's Convertible Division. Joined the sanctioning body's premier series in 1960 and won 25 NASCAR Winston Cup races and 19 poles in 230 starts. Won two titles in 1962 and 1963. 1962 title was first for car owner Bud Moore. 1963 title based on consistency with 35 top-ten finishes in 53 starts.

LeeRoy Yarbrough had confidence that rivals said bordered on arrogance. But no one questioned his ability.

Yarbrough could get a race car running at the fastest speed it possibly could reach.

"I'll drive anything if it's got wheels and can get me to the front," he said. And he wasn't kidding.

"LeeRoy drove a car like he was a bull chasing a red cape," a competitor once remarked.

Yarbrough charged to the front any time it was humanly possible—whether it be a NASCAR Winston Cup race, the Indy 500, or a Sportsman race.

"Racing at Indy is great," Yarbrough said after one of his first Indy 500s. "But I didn't want to win here any more than I wanted to win those races on short tracks back home when I was growing up. I want to lead and win all the time. I don't care where."

Yarbrough won only 14 races in 198 NASCAR Winston Cup starts. But he led a total of 66 races.

And his 1969 season was one of the greatest in NASCAR Winston Cup history. He won 7 races—all on superspeedways. Until then, no driver had won more than 4 superspeedway races in a season.

Even winning didn't completely satisfy Yarbrough.

"I want to win fast," he once said. Again, he meant it.

LeeRoy Yarbrough

Born: September 17, 1938 (d. 1984)
Hometown: Jacksonville, Florida
The File: At the age of fourteen, LeeRoy lied about his age to get his racing license and launched a hard-charging career. After winning 52 races in one year at a local track, began racing NASCAR events at age twenty-one. Won 37 Sportsman races at NASCAR tracks in 1962. In 1969, had one of the greatest seasons in NASCAR Winston Cup history. Won 7 races and had 21 top-10 finishes to earn him a record $193,211. All 7 wins were on superspeedways, including a sweep of the Daytona 500, Coca-Cola 600 at Charlotte, and Southern 500 at Darlington.

"LeeRoy had determination and a no-quit attitude. He's right at the top of the list of the all-time great race drivers."

—JUNIOR JOHNSON

Four of NASCAR's Fifty Greatest Drivers wage a bumper-to-bumper battle for the lead in one of NASCAR's greatest races—the 1976 Daytona 500. David Pearson narrowly leads A.J. Foyt with Richard Petty and Buddy Baker in pursuit. Pearson's Mercury emerged from the smoke of a last-turn collision with Petty's Dodge to win the race.

Babe Ruth put baseball on the map. Michael Jordan made the world take notice of the NBA. And before Wayne Gretzky, few paid attention to the NHL.

Great stars propel sports to new heights.

Just when NASCAR was ready for a new superstar, a giant appeared in Richard Petty. And he wasn't alone. The 1960s and early 1970s featured some of the greatest drivers—and the greatest races—in NASCAR history.

Petty, along with David Pearson, Bobby Allison, Buddy Baker, Cale Yarborough, Bobby Isaac, and more, became the focus.

During NASCAR's formative years, the stars were the cars. What won on Sunday sold on Monday.

Petty would change all that. He hit his stride just as the general public began taking notice of NASCAR. He became NASCAR's biggest superstar—a national icon.

And as rivals like Pearson, the Allison brothers, and Yarborough pushed Petty into the record books, NASCAR racing took off, swept along in the draft of its great drivers.

"Looking back, I think the days of Petty and Pearson were very special for the sport," Darrell Waltrip said. "They became heroes to an awful lot of people, many of whom weren't car racing fans.

"They opened doors for the sport and welcomed the rest of us in."

Petty's record of 200 NASCAR Winston Cup victories might stand forever. Pearson ranks second on the all-time chart with 105 wins.

But more than their victories, it was their head-to-head duels—brought to a climax by the 1976 Daytona 500—that brought new fans to the sport and left even the most ardent NASCAR partisan emotionally drained.

"Racing David was like punching a mountain lion in the nose," Petty said. "He was never going to let you get away. You couldn't find a place to hide. David was stalking you every second of the race."

"Petty had every corner of the sport covered," said Pearson. "He was a great driver and more. He knew cars and he knew how to drive. And he knew how to put a team and a car together. Those Petty guys were so smart."

Petty, "the King"—handsome, personable, charismatic—a seven-time NASCAR Winston Cup champion. No one has ever been better than Petty was during the 1967 season when he had twenty-seven wins, including a run of ten straight.

Pearson, "the Silver Fox"—cunning, tenacious and fast—was an even bet against Petty anytime they met on a superspeedway.

"Every time we hooked up, you knew it was going to be exciting and come right down to that last turn," said Petty.

Which is exactly what happened in the 1976 Daytona 500, which was also the first time that the finish of NASCAR's premier race was shown live on national television. They were side by side entering the final turn of the 200th and last lap with Pearson high and Petty diving low for the pass. They touched. They spun. Petty crashed hard into the outside wall. Pearson kept his heavily damaged car running down on the apron and somehow took the checkered flag.

It was but one battle of many that brought attention to other NASCAR stories.

The new Talladega Superspeedway combined with the sleek Dodge Daytonas and Plymouth Superbirds produced mind-boggling speeds. On March 24, 1970, Buddy Baker hit 200.447 mph at Talladega.

Richie Evans and Jerry Cook were dominating the NASCAR Modified Division.

"It was a time of heroes," said Bobby Allison. "It was the heyday of a lot of great drivers."

Red Farmer was more than the first member of NASCAR's famed "Alabama Gang." He was the Papa Bear.

Bobby Allison was Farmer's protégé. And when Allison was out on the road seeing to his NASCAR Winston Cup career, Farmer was back home watching over the formative days of son Davey Allison's driving career.

Farmer was quite a driver in his own right.

He won three straight NASCAR Busch Series, Grand National Division titles (1969–71) plus the 1956 NASCAR Modified title. Overall, Farmer has won close to seven hundred races in a career that began in the early 1950s and continued on into the 1990s. During the '50s and '60s, Farmer would race up to four and five times a week.

He was a short-track phenom who prided himself on being able to quickly pick up the nuances of a surface he had never run on before.

Farmer was one of those men who believed strongly that the more you raced, the better you ran. He was a very smart, very smooth driver, and rivals would go to him for answers to the questions that perplex racers.

"He knows how to set a car up on a short track better than anyone I've ever seen," said Bobby Allison. "He has a feel. And he knew how to teach that information to others."

"Red played an important role in our successes. He taught me a lot," said Neil Bonnett. "And when I needed to bounce something off someone, I turned to Red."

Although his racing career has now ended, Farmer continues to serve as a crew chief on the Alabama circuits that he once dominated.

Born: October 15, 1932
Hometown: Hueytown, Alabama
The File: Although born in Hialeah, Florida, Farmer established roots in Hueytown where he became the original member of the "Alabama Gang." Won three straight NASCAR Busch Series, Grand National Division titles (1969–71). Was the NASCAR Modified Division champion in 1956. Made 36 NASCAR Winston Cup starts with his best finish, a fourth place in the 1968 Middle Georgia 500.

"I learned a lot about racing from Red, who I always thought was one of the best short-track drivers I've ever seen."

—BOBBY ALLISON

Red Farmer

Some drivers are competitive.

Others are combative.

Bobby Allison was combative—anywhere, all the time.

Few NASCAR Winston Cup drivers threw so much of their heart and soul into racing as Bobby Allison did. And his desire to race—and win—extended far beyond the boundaries of the elite NASCAR Winston Cup Series.

An off-weekend would find Bobby at a remote half-mile—just for the fun of it—or helping a promoter who had befriended Bobby along the way.

Allison is known as one of NASCAR's greatest ambassadors, although that description could surprise those who dueled with him on the track for a position.

"I like to shake hands and smile with people off the track," Allison said during a visit to a small Southern California oval in the early 1980s.

"But don't let that fool you."

Those who raced him weren't fooled.

Allison played push-and-shove with everyone from Curtis Turner to Richard Petty to Darrell Waltrip. Often, Allison was running right there with the best of them despite spending much of his career in second-echelon equipment.

"I believe if I'm even going into the last lap, I'll win," Allison once said. "I will find a way or I'll crash."

Bobby Allison

"If there's anybody tougher or more determined than Bobby, I've never met them."

—NEIL BONNETT

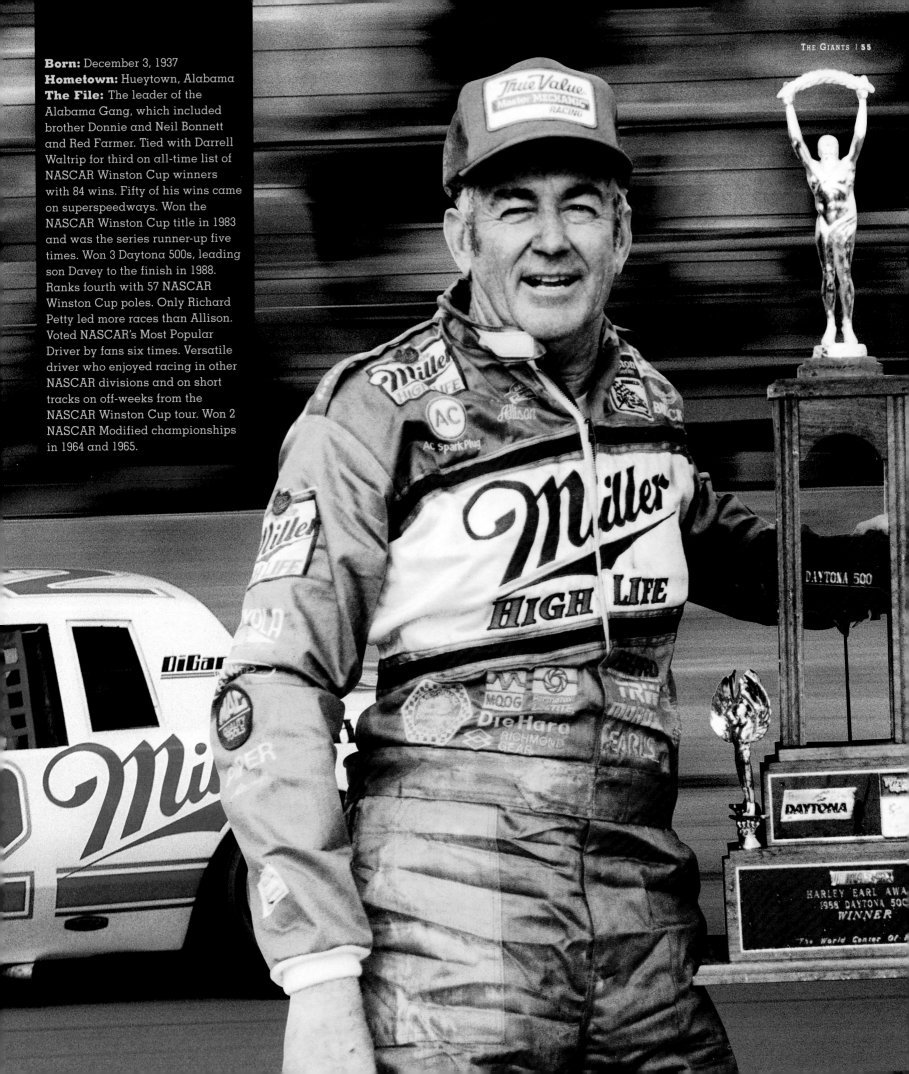

Born: December 3, 1937
Hometown: Hueytown, Alabama
The File: The leader of the Alabama Gang, which included brother Donnie and Neil Bonnett and Red Farmer. Tied with Darrell Waltrip for third on all-time list of NASCAR Winston Cup winners with 84 wins. Fifty of his wins came on superspeedways. Won the NASCAR Winston Cup title in 1983 and was the series runner-up five times. Won 3 Daytona 500s, leading son Davey to the finish in 1988. Ranks fourth with 57 NASCAR Winston Cup poles. Only Richard Petty led more races than Allison. Voted NASCAR's Most Popular Driver by fans six times. Versatile driver who enjoyed racing in other NASCAR divisions and on short tracks on off-weeks from the NASCAR Winston Cup tour. Won 2 NASCAR Modified championships in 1964 and 1965.

Born: January 25, 1941
Hometown: Charlotte, North Carolina
The File: Dubbed "Bigfoot" by his peers for his pedal-to-the-metal style, Baker was one of the fastest drivers ever to tour a superspeedway. First driver to break the 200-mph barrier on March 24, 1970, at Talladega Superspeedway (200.447 mph) in a winged Dodge Daytona. Won the fastest Daytona 500 ever, averaging 177.602 mph in an Oldsmobile in 1980. Won consecutive Coca-Cola 600s at Charlotte in 1972–73. Six of 19 career wins and 7 pole victories came on the high banks at Daytona and Talladega. Ranks ninth on the NASCAR Winston Cup list of top-five (202) and top-ten (311) finishes. Ranks 10th in career pole positions with 40.

The son of two-time NASCAR Winston Cup Series champion Buck Baker, Buddy had a big smile and a big foot.

Few drivers were as fast as Baker at NASCAR's two fastest tracks—Daytona and Talladega.

Buddy Baker

"If Buddy had a car under him, nobody could outdrive him when it came to Daytona and Talladega," said car owner Bud Moore.

The sentiment was echoed by longtime rival Bobby Allison: "Going down those long backstretches at Daytona and Talladega, Buddy was a blur."

Baker was flat-out fast on the track. He was the first NASCAR driver to top 200 mph. In 1980, he averaged 177.602 mph to win the fastest Daytona 500 ever. The previous season, Baker won both Daytona poles.

"Buddy was as good as anyone I've ever seen at Daytona and Talladega," said car owner Leonard Wood.

But his hard-charging, aggressive nature on the track was the opposite of his off-the-track persona.

Witty and friendly, Baker easily moved from the cockpit to the broadcast booth as a commentator after retiring as a driver in 1994.

"Buddy is a guy who loved to drive a race car," said crew chief Waddell Wilson. "And he was a lot of fun to be around. Off the track, he was one of everyone's favorite people."

"When Buddy was hooked up on a superspeedway, it was almost impossible to hold onto him."

—DARRELL WALTRIP

"Jerry and I joked that we put Rome, New York, on the map. But I don't think it was a joke. For two guys from a small town, we won a lot of races." —RICHIE EVANS

Born: June 20, 1943
Hometown: Lockport, New York
The File: Cook's twenty-year racing career was spent in the NASCAR Modified Division. Won six titles, including four straight from 1974–77 after winning his first two season championships in 1971 and 1972. Won 342 races in 1,474 career modified starts. Finished in the top ten in an astounding 85 percent of his races.

For all the victories and championships, when Jerry Cook's racing career ended October, 11, 1982, at Martinsville, Virginia, it was with a touch of irony.

Throughout his career, Cook drove No. 38. And in that final race, he went out on the 38th lap with engine problems. His final finish: 38th.

But 38 was a number that rivals and fans became used to seeing at the front of NASCAR Modified Division races during Cook's storied twenty-year career.

Cook won 6 NASCAR Modified Division season championships and 342 races in the division. He and Rome, New York, neighbor/rival Richie Evans

won 15 straight NASCAR Modified Division championships between them from 1971 to 1985.

Before Cook won his first title in 1971, he had twice finished second in the division. He also finished second to Evans three times before retiring to become the director of the tour he once dominated.

Even more impressive than Cook's win total was his ability to run near the top while competing as many as three and four times a week. During his six championship seasons, Cook averaged 87 NASCAR Modified races a season. He finished in the top ten in 81 percent of those starts and ran among the top five 60 percent of the time.

"I always wanted to win," said Cook. "But I never wanted to go home without something to show for racing."

Jerry Cook

David Pearson

David Pearson was a smart race car driver. Crafty. Calculating. Cunning. Cool.

When he had to be fast, Pearson was as fast as anyone.

But his style was to save his equipment early in races—usually after winning the pole—then charge late.

"You couldn't make David race you on the tenth or the one-hundredth lap," said Bobby Allison, one of Pearson's fiercest rivals. "But when they got that checkered flag out, he was ready to go."

Pearson raced on his terms—not his rivals'.

"He worked hard at making it look easy," said Ned Jarrett. "He took care of his equipment. He knew when to race hard and when not to. And he was smart."

The 1974 Firecracker 400 at Daytona was an example of Pearson at his best. Petty was stalking race leader Pearson and setting "the Silver Fox" up for a slingshot pass entering the final lap. As they approached the white flag, Pearson slowed and dropped low on the track as Petty flew past.

Pearson had flipped off his ignition for a split second, then refired. The hunter was now the hunted. Pearson passed Petty on the final turn for the win.

"David was just so smooth. He made it look easy," said Leonard Wood. "He knew exactly what he could do with a car and when he could do it. And before you'd know it, he'd run you into the ground."

"Pearson was the best driver who ever lived. There's no doubt about it. He could drive any kind of car on any kind of track." —COTTON OWENS

Born: December 22, 1934
Home: Spartanburg, South Carolina
The File: Dubbed "the Silver Fox" for his driving style as well as his prematurely graying hair, Pearson is considered among the most cunning of drivers. Ran for NASCAR Winston Cup championship honors only five times and won three titles in 1966, 1968, and 1969. His 105 career NASCAR Winston Cup wins is second only to Richard Petty's 200, but Pearson started only 574 races—less than half as many as Petty. Also ranks second with 113 career poles. Won 64 races on superspeedways. Won 11 of the 18 races he entered in 1973 and a total of 43 races during 1972–79 while driving for the Wood Brothers. Won 18 percent of his starts and finished in the top five 52 percent of the time.

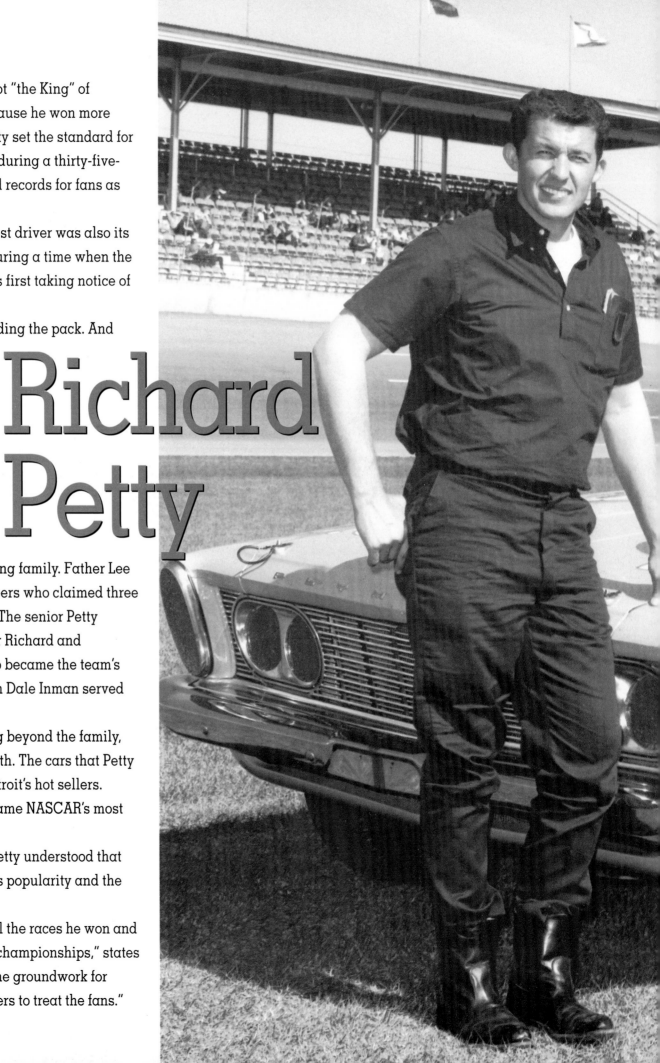

Richard Petty is not "the King" of NASCAR racing simply because he won more races than anyone else. Petty set the standard for drivers on and off the track during a thirty-five-year career that established records for fans as well as victories.

NASCAR's winningest driver was also its most popular personality during a time when the general sporting public was first taking notice of NASCAR.

There was Petty leading the pack. And there was Petty—with his signature dark glasses, oversized cowboy hat, and toothy grin—signing autographs and doing interviews until dark had descended on yet another of his 1,184 NASCAR Winston Cup outings.

Richard Petty

He came from a racing family. Father Lee was one of NASCAR's pioneers who claimed three championships of his own. The senior Petty formed Petty Enterprises for Richard and youngest son, Maurice, who became the team's engine builder while cousin Dale Inman served as crew chief.

But Petty took racing beyond the family, and NASCAR out of the South. The cars that Petty drove to victory became Detroit's hot sellers. No. 43 and "Petty Blue" became NASCAR's most identifiable trademarks.

More importantly, Petty understood that the fans were the core of his popularity and the heart of racing itself.

"His legacy is not all the races he won and all the trophies and all the championships," states son Kyle. "It's how he laid the groundwork for NASCAR Winston Cup drivers to treat the fans."

"*There is only one Richard Petty. There's only ever been one. There will only ever be one.*"

—DALE EARNHARDT

Born: July 2, 1937
Hometown: Level Cross, North Carolina
The File: Won 7 NASCAR Winston Cup titles (1964, 1967, 1971, 1972, 1974, 1975, 1979) and 200 races. Started 1,184 with 126 poles, 599 race leads, and 555 top-five finishes. Completed 307,836 laps and led 52,194 of them. Career spanned 35 seasons and his successes helped propel NASCAR into the spotlight. Best season also considered the best in NASCAR Winston Cup history. In 1967, won 27 of the season's 48 races—including a record 10 straight—and finished second 7 times. Drove 303,662 miles in NASCAR Winston Cup races.

Cale Yarborough

When Cale Yarborough was eleven years old, he sneaked under the fence at Darlington to see the first Southern 500. Seven years later, he sneaked in again. To drive. Under age. Anything you told Yarborough he couldn't do—he'd give it a try. He believed he could do it all.

Before he had reached maturity, Yarborough was struck by a rattlesnake and lightning, and had wrestled an alligator. He took up skydiving and went from being a high school football star directly to playing for a semipro team. Becoming a race car driver was a gimme.

And as a driver, he became one of the hardest chargers the sport has ever seen. Richard Petty was smooth. David Pearson was smart. Bobby Allison was determined. Cale Yarborough was tough.

If you beat him, you had a better car. You didn't outdrive him or outlast him.

"I don't know if there's ever been an athlete who had that outlook on the last ten laps that Cale Yarborough had," said Buddy Baker. "He didn't give up until the last inch of the race was over."

"Cale jumped in the car and pushed the throttle to the floor before he switched it on," Bobby Allison once noted. "When the green fell, he locked the throttle on 'kill,' gritted his teeth, and held on."

It is said that car owner Junior Johnson once instructed Yarborough: "Just bring me back the steering wheel." Yarborough brought Johnson three straight titles.

Born: March 27, 1939
Hometown: Timmonsville, South Carolina
The File: Yarborough is the only driver to win 3 consecutive NASCAR Winston Cup championships (1976, 1977, 1978). Ranks fifth with 83 career wins, third with 70 poles, and is tied for third with 47 superspeedway wins. Ranks No. 2 in laps led (31,776) and fifth in races led (340 out of 559 starts). Won 15 percent of all starts. Four-time winner of the Daytona 500 (including back-to-back victories in 1983–84) and five-time winner of Southern 500 at Darlington Raceway. Four Daytona 500 wins are second only to Richard Petty. First driver to qualify at over 200 mph (201.848) for Daytona 500 in 1984. Won 14 poles in 1980 and 5 straight races in 1976.

"Let me put it this way: Cale ran that thing wide open no matter whether it had two wheels, three wheels, four wheels, or bent fenders. That made him a very fierce competitor."

—RICHARD PETTY

Born: July 23, 1941 (d. 1985)
Hometown: Rome, New York
The File: Evans won more than 500 races during his career. Called "the King of Modifieds." Won 9 NASCAR Modified Division season championships—the first in 1973, then a remarkable 8 straight from 1978 to 1985. Evans was also the NASCAR Winston Racing Series's Northeast Region champion four straight years (1982–85). An example of Evans' domination was the 1979 season when he won 37 of the 60 NASCAR Modified Division races he started and had 54 top-five finishes.

"Evans knew how to race a modified as good as any driver I've ever seen. That was his home." —GEOFF BODINE

Richie Evans

Those who knew Richie Evans and those who saw him drive are convinced that Evans would have been a winner on the NASCAR Winston Cup tour—had he ever wanted to run on that circuit.

But that wasn't what Evans wanted.

His home was the NASCAR Modified Division. And he was arguably the greatest Modified driver who ever rolled his car onto a short track.

Evans had a style that was perfectly suited to short-track and Modified racing. He was very aggressive. And he knew how to hustle a car in and out of the tight turns.

A number of drivers raced Evans in NASCAR's Modified and Sportsman classes en route to the NASCAR Winston Cup Series. But not many moved on with a winning record against Evans.

Evans was also involved in one of the greatest finishes in NASCAR history. In the Dogwood Classic Modified race at Martinsville in 1981, Evans and Geoff Bodine slammed together coming off the final turn. Evans' car climbed sideways onto the outside retaining wall. Evans never lifted off the throttle and bounced along the wall on three wheels to take the checkered flag.

Early in the 1980s, several teams approached Evans about driving in the NASCAR Winston Cup Series. But he declined. Evans was making excellent money as NASCAR's "King of Modifieds."

"Ray might have been one of the best of a special breed. They were really good drivers on small tracks. They knew every trick about where they were running. If they caught you on their track, you could be in big trouble."

—BOBBY ALLISON

Ray Hendrick

Ray Hendrick ran anywhere and everywhere. He raced for twenty-nine seasons. There were times when he raced four and five times a week. And he raced hard.

But the Virginian never raced long enough in any one series to win a national NASCAR championship.

During a career that began in 1956, Hendrick ran NASCAR Modified and Sportsman classes. Many of his races were close to his Richmond, Virginia, home at Southside Speedway in Richmond, at Langley Speedway in Newport News, and at South Boston Speedway.

But he also toured and once held the record for most wins at Martinsville Speedway.

During his travels, Hendrick's very aggressive style made more than a few enemies among the competition. But track promoters loved him; a match of Hendrick versus anyone was guaranteed to be exciting.

Born: April 1, 1929 (d. 1990)
Hometown: Richmond, Virginia
The File: Hendrick spent 29 years on the track, most of it racing in NASCAR's Modified and Sportsman divisions. Records indicate Hendrick won as many as 712 main events at a large number and wide variety of short tracks. Never ran a full NASCAR Winston Cup campaign. Made only 17 career NASCAR Winston Cup starts with 2 top-five finishes and 6 top-tens.

At the age of twelve, Bobby Isaac took a break from school to go to work in a sawmill. He needed shoes.

"I was from a large family and it was a struggle," Isaac once recalled. "I was on my own and it was cold in the winter and I didn't have shoes. We'd go barefoot as long as we could because it made your feet tough."

Tough is what Bobby Isaac was. Tough and fast.

Early in his racing career, his bad temper combined with an aggressive driving style led to more than one off-the-track altercation following a short-track race.

By the time he reached the NASCAR Winston Cup circuit, Isaac had harnessed that temper and turned it into a drive that made him one of the hardest-charging drivers the sport has ever seen.

The name of Bobby Isaac was synonymous with speed. In 1964, during his first regular season on the NASCAR Winston Cup circuit, Isaac led every race he entered.

How appropriate that in the late 1960s and early 1970s he would hook up with the futuristic high-winged Dodge Daytonas. In 1969, Isaac set a single-season NASCAR Winston Cup record by claiming twenty poles. After clinching his only NASCAR Winston Cup title in 1970, he set a record with a lap of 201.104 mph in a closed-course test at Talladega.

Although he ranks fifteenth in NASCAR Winston Cup victories with 37, Isaac ranks seventh with 13,229 laps led and sixth with 50 poles.

Bobby Isaac

"Bobby Isaac was flat-out fast."

—Cale Yarborough

Born: August 1, 1932 (d. 1977)
Hometown: Catawba, North Carolina
The File: Bobby won 37 races in a fifteen-year NASCAR Winston Cup career that numbered 308 races. Best known for his achievements during the 1970 season. Driving one of the exotic, high-winged Dodge Daytonas, won 11 races to claim the NASCAR Winston Cup title. Won 50 poles in his career to rank sixth on the all-time list. He also ranks fifteenth among NASCAR Winston Cup race winners.

Tim Richmond (27), with Bobby Allison (22) in tow, goes high on the banking at Daytona International Speedway to pass Darrell Waltrip (11).

The biggest boost to NASCAR in the late 1970s and early 1980s was not new tracks and faster cars.

It was television.

"This sport was perfect for television, but no one in television could see that for a long time," driver-turned-commentator Benny Parsons said.

"When the sport hit the tube, both sides won."

Television executives knew NASCAR's action was perfectly suited to their medium. What they didn't know until they started covering races was that NASCAR's superstars were also ready-made television personalities.

Drivers like Darrell Waltrip, Tim Richmond, Parsons, and Alan Kulwicki not only won races, they had personalities that blossomed on the small screen.

The cameras also loved the folksy charisma of a Richard Petty and the down-home qualities of drivers like Harry Gant and Neil Bonnett.

"Drivers are great for television," said Waltrip. "Hand us a microphone and put us in front of the camera and we'll have something to say. It just took television awhile to find this out. I think TV worried that we'd be an incoherent glob of grime after climbing out of the cockpit after a five-hundred-mile race."

Just the opposite was true. By the time the cameras found NASCAR, the great drivers had already discovered that fans and sponsors appreciated public speaking skills almost as much as wins.

And if television needed the perfect race to launch start-to-finish coverage, they found it with the 1979 Daytona 500.

Heading down the backstretch for the last time, Cale Yarborough and Donnie

Allison battled for the lead, bumping each other as their cars headed into the third turn—where they crashed and slid off into the infield. As their cars came to a stop in the grass, Richard Petty sped around for the unexpected victory. It wasn't over, however. With the cameras split between the finish line and the crash scene, Yarborough engaged Bobby Allison, who had come to the aid of his brother, in a brief but spirited fight.

In short order, thanks to the expansion of cable networks, every NASCAR Winston Cup race was shown live on television. That coverage has spread to the NASCAR Busch Series and NASCAR Craftsman Truck Series.

But to make television work, NASCAR needed drivers who worked well on television.

Waltrip was the right man in the right place in the right time. He won twenty-four races and back-to-back championships in 1981–82 just as NASCAR was going live across the land.

Waltrip was handsome, animated, and verbal: a perfect television package.

"NASCAR couldn't have handpicked a better champion for their earliest years on television," said Ned Jarrett, another driver-turned-commentator. "Darrell understood television. And the camera loved him. More importantly, Darrell showed other NASCAR drivers how to make television work for the sport."

And if Waltrip was a winner with the camera, the era produced a giant who was a winner in every way—Earnhardt. With the cameras rolling, Earnhardt raced to seven NASCAR Winston Cup titles, equalling a Petty record that had once seemed unapproachable.

"Everything took off in the 1980s," said Petty. "I never thought it would get that big. But television took our story to every corner of the country. People liked what they saw. And they started coming to races in record numbers.

"It's pretty amazing how it all came together."

A.J. Foyt

You name it and A.J. Foyt raced it.

Midgets, sprint cars, open-wheel roadsters, sports cars, rear-engined championship cars, and stock cars: A.J. raced them all. And he raced them everywhere from Indianapolis to Le Mans and from the high-banks and the road course at Daytona International Speedway.

Foyt always had a special place in his heart for NASCAR and the NASCAR Winston Cup Series.

Beginning in 1963 when he ran third in his NASCAR debut at the Daytona 500, Foyt made 128 NASCAR Winston Cup starts in a run that spanned four decades. Due to his Indy-car commitments, he never made more than seven starts in any single season. His first NASCAR Winston Cup victory came in the 1964 Firecracker 400 at Daytona.

Foyt's most memorable seasons on the NASCAR circuit were 1971 and 1972 while driving the Wood Brothers' Mercury. In seven starts in 1971, Foyt had two wins, two poles, and four top-five finishes. He opened the 1972 season by winning the Daytona 500 and finished with two wins, three poles, and five top-five finishes in six starts.

"We got along with A.J. because we gave a one-hundred percent effort and so did he. A.J. was one of the best drivers we ever had," said Glen Wood.

Foyt's final NASCAR Winston Cup outing was the inaugural running of the Brickyard 400 at the Indianapolis Motor Speedway in 1994.

> *"I've always respected A.J. for what he could do in any type of a car—an open wheel car, a stock car, or a sports car. He had a gift."* —RICHARD PETTY

Born: January 16, 1935
Hometown: Houston, Texas
The File: Although better known for his four wins in the Indy 500, Foyt also made 128 NASCAR Winston Cup starts. First victory came in the 1964 Firecracker 400 at Daytona in his 10th start. Won the Daytona 500 in 1972, joining Mario Andretti as the only two men to win both the Daytona and Indianapolis 500s. Had seven NASCAR Winston Cup wins. Also won the 24 Hours of Daytona endurance sports car race twice.

Born: July 12, 1941
Hometown: Detroit, Michigan
The File: Parsons won his only NASCAR Winston Cup championship in 1973. Won 20 NASCAR Winston Cup races and 20 poles. Made 526 starts in a twenty-one-year career. Biggest wins were in the 1975 Daytona 500 and 1980 Coca-Cola 600 at Charlotte. Was the first NASCAR Winston Cup driver to qualify at over 200 mph for the 1982 Winston 500 at Talladega. Now a respected radio and television analyst of NASCAR Winston Cup racing.

"Benny could drive a car and spin a yarn. He was a natural for the broadcast booth." —CAR OWNER BUD MOORE

Benny Parsons

Every time he'd win a race, Benny Parsons' past would become part of the story.

Here was a man who went from driving taxicabs in Detroit, Michigan, to racing on the NASCAR Winston Cup tour. But the story was incomplete.

Benny's father owned the taxi company. And, yes, Parsons would drive at times. But he did a lot of other things. But it was a good story—and Parsons was always a good story.

And if he wasn't providing one through his deeds on the track, he was telling them in the pits and garages. "Benny could get you laughing so hard you'd forget your other business," Neil Bonnett recalled. "He'd start spinning those yarns and you'd forget you had work to do."

It was only natural that after his driving career ended in 1988 that Parsons would be sought out by television to add his folksy stories and racing knowledge to telecasts of NASCAR Winston Cup racing.

"I loved the driving," says Parsons. "But I have to admit that I might be better suited to what I'm doing today—talking."

Once again, Benny was right on the mark.

Neil Bonnett

Fast and friendly, Neil Bonnett always had a nice word for the fans who crowded around NASCAR garages.

And usually the word had a laugh attached. Speed and humor. Few drivers matched Bonnett's ability to tie the two together.

"The biggest thing about Neil was his smile," Dale Earnhardt said of his close friend. "It came from deep inside. And we loved his sense of humor."

Bonnett was as quick with a quip as he was with a car.

Once he was asked why he attached a pair of 105-horsepower outboard engines to his little bass-fishing boat. "Well," said Bonnett, "when you hook into one of those suckers at eighty miles an hour it takes the fight right out of 'em."

Bonnett drove for some of the top NASCAR Winston Cup teams during his career. He won the first of his two straight Coca-Cola 600s at Charlotte driving for the Wood Brothers and finished a career-high fourth in the 1985 Winston Cup standings driving for Junior Johnson.

"Neil was the type of person who threw himself into whatever he was doing," said Red Farmer. "Absolutely loved to race. But he also loved the opportunities that racing brought to him. He loved being around people."

"Neil was a great driver. He was also as good a friend as anyone could ever find. Times with Neil were always special."

—DALE EARNHARDT

Born: July 30, 1946 (d. 1994)
Hometown: Bessemer, Alabama
The File: Bonnett was a member of the Alabama Gang that included the Allisons and Red Farmer. Won eighteen races in a seventeen-year NASCAR Winston Cup career. Best season finish came in 1985 when he finished fourth and teammate Darrell Waltrip won the NASCAR Winston Cup title. Scored back-to-back wins in NASCAR's longest race: the Coca-Cola 600 at Charlotte (1982 and 1983). Also won consecutive Busch Clash races at Daytona in 1983–84.

Jack Ingram

Jack Ingram was a very important figure in NASCAR during a time of change.

Ingram had already won three straight NASCAR Late Model Sportsman division titles in the 1970s when NASCAR decided to restructure its second series before the 1982 season.

Like the NASCAR Winston Cup Series a decade earlier, the Sportsman division got a new name—NASCAR Busch Series, Grand National Division—and a revised schedule.

The length of the season was shortened from its fifty- to sixty-race schedule while its exposure was increased through more races at major tracks and superspeedways.

As a three-time champion and one of the more popular Sportsman drivers, Ingram was counted on to help launch the new division. He did so by winning the inaugural title in 1982 and claiming two of the first four season championships.

On the track, Ingram was a tough, aggressive driver who didn't mind swapping paint while battling for a position. He excelled on the shorter ovals and his roots were in the short, North Carolina ovals at his hometown, Asheville, and at Hickory.

As the Sportsman/Grand National series grew, Ingram gained a national sponsor and had no need to gamble on a NASCAR Winston Cup ride. He was already a national champion.

"There are some guys out there who could have won on the Winston Cup level if they had raced there," said Red Farmer. "Ingram was one of those drivers."

> *"Jack was one tough racer. He didn't like to lose. And while he did most of his racing on short tracks, he was good wherever we went."*
>
> —HARRY GANT

Born: December 28, 1938
Hometown: Asheville, North Carolina
The File: Ingram spent his entire career in the NASCAR Busch Series. Won three straight titles (1972–74) when the series was known as the NASCAR Late Model Sportsman Division. Final two season championships came in 1982 and 1985 after the tour had been reorganized into the NASCAR Busch Series. Made 275 starts in the division and won 31 races, which was a record until 1997.

Oregon is a long way from Daytona Beach, Florida. It's also a long haul from the southern tip of Mexico.

But those are the lengths that Hershel McGriff would travel to race.

The Oregon lumberman loved stock car racing. So much so that he assisted bringing NASCAR out west by helping form—and campaign—on the NASCAR Winston West Series.

Every year, McGriff would hook up with his friends at Ontario Motor Speedway and Riverside International Raceway until those tracks closed. He made a couple of runs at Sears Point Raceway.

A friend of Bill France Sr., McGriff got his start in racing on September 16, 1945, on a track in Portland, Oregon, near his hometown. McGriff has forgotten what kind of car he drove. "But three of the wheels broke and I finished sixteenth," he recalls.

He traveled south in 1950 and raced in the first Southern 500 at Darlington, finishing ninth. He also won the first Pan-American Road Race that year driving a 1950 Oldsmobile. In 1954, McGriff spent his only full season on the NASCAR Winston Cup tour, scoring his only four NASCAR Winston Cup wins and finishing sixth in points.

McGriff never again raced more than five NASCAR Winston Cup events in any season—although he raced in at least one event for twenty-eight years.

McGriff raced—and won—in six different decades.

"Hershel was there in the early days and he's still racing and running hard. I always admired his desire and attitude in addition to his skill."

—MARVIN PANCH

Hershel McGriff

Born: December 14, 1927
Hometown: Bridal Veil, Oregon
The File: Became one of NASCAR's oldest champions in 1986 when he won the NASCAR Winston West Series title at age fifty-eight. First race was in 1945 and he is one of few men who can claim to racing in six different decades. First major victory was in the 2,135-mile Pan-American Road Race of 1950. Finished ninth in the inaugural Southern 500 at Darlington that same year. Competed in 1954 NASCAR Winston Cup Series, winning four races and placing sixth in points.

Tough. Tenacious. Independent. Strong-willed. Stubborn. Aggressive.

All are adjectives used over the years to describe Geoff Bodine, who broke through barriers to battle his way to the NASCAR Winston Cup Series.

"I want to be my own boss and answer only to myself," Bodine said.

His interests are varied. Upset with the United States's struggles in bobsledding in the Olympic Games, Bodine developed a new bobsled in 1994 and funded his own entry.

But his life has centered around racing since he first began driving micro-midgets near his upstate New York home at the age of six.

Bodine first drew national attention on NASCAR's Modified circuit in the 1970s while battling the likes of Jerry Cook and Richie Evans. He advanced to the NASCAR Busch Series where he won six races.

In 1982 he was the NASCAR Winston Cup Rookie of the Year and won his first three races in 1984 while teamed with rookie car owner Rick Hendrick.

Bodine fulfilled his dream to be his own boss midway through the 1993 season when he bought the team of the late Alan Kulwicki. Bodine campaigned for four years as an owner-driver and won four races driving for himself.

Geoff Bodine

"When I first saw him driving modifieds, I thought, 'This is a guy who could go places.'"—JERRY COOK

Born: April 18, 1949
Hometown: Chemung, New York
The File: Finished in the top ten in the final NASCAR Winston Cup standings five times with a third-place finish in 1990 while driving for Junior Johnson. Was fifth in 1985 and sixth in 1988 while driving for Rick Hendrick. Bought the team of the late Alan Kulwicki during 1993 season and ran for four-plus years as an owner-driver, scoring four wins. Before NASCAR Winston Cup career, was named the 1977 runner-up in points in the NASCAR Modified Division and had six wins in the NASCAR Busch Series.

Harry Gant

Harry Gant is one of the most popular drivers ever to enter a NASCAR garage.

"Harry was one of those guys that you just wanted to see good things happen to," said Rusty Wallace.

And in September of 1991, good things happened to Gant. Four good things—in a row.

On consecutive racing Sundays, Gant won NASCAR Winston Cup races at Darlington, South Carolina; Richmond, Virginia; Dover, Delaware; and Martinsville, Virginia, to tie a modern-era (1972 to the present) four straight victories. He also won two NASCAR Busch Series races during the run.

He was fifty-one at the time. A year later, he eclipsed Bobby Allison to become the oldest driver ever to win a NASCAR Winston Cup race. It was the eighteenth victory of a career that didn't begin until he was thirty-nine.

"A lot of people asked me if I had wished my career started when I was younger," Gant said before his final race. "Sure. But I look at it this way: How lucky was I that I could start a career at thirty-nine."

"If Harry had started earlier, he would have won a lot of championships," said crew chief Andy Petree. "The thing about Harry, he is the toughest human being who ever lived to drive a race car. He was as strong at the end of the race as he was at the start. And Harry was usually one of the oldest guys out there."

"Harry was one driver that other drivers pulled for. There was never a sad face when Harry won."
—TERRY LABONTE

Born: January 10, 1940
Home: Taylorsville,
North Carolina
The File: Gant had already had a successful short-track career by the time he joined the NASCAR Winston Cup Series in 1979 as a thirty-nine-year-old rookie. On August 16, 1992, on the high-banked, two-mile oval at Michigan, became the oldest driver ever to win a NASCAR Winston Cup race at fifty-two. In between, won 18 races in 474 starts and finished as high as second in series in 1984. He finished in the top ten 8 times.

Alan Kulwicki was different.

He was not southern-bred. He had not grown up around racetracks as a way of life.

He was a quiet, devout Catholic from Wisconsin with a stubborn streak. He was going to do it his way— even if it meant doing everything himself. Which is really how he wanted to do it.

Armed with a college degree and a love of mechanics as well as racing, Kulwicki ran his own team. He managed. He drove. And he plunged under the car after practice sessions to adjust the springs.

Other teams had years of experience. Kulwicki had brains and drive—both of which he pushed long into the night. Other NASCAR Winston Cup drivers went to dinner. Kulwicki went back to work with his small team of family and friends that made up his crew.

"Is this a hard way to do it?" Kulwicki once asked rhetorically. "Yes.

"But it's my way—maybe the only way that it will work for me. To succeed, I have to know how I succeeded. That's how it will be meaningful."

After seven seasons of battling the bigger teams, it all came together for Kulwicki in 1992. He won the NASCAR Winston Cup title by a mere ten points over Bill Elliott.

"Not too many of us figure it out on our own. Alan did," said Terry Labonte. "He knew everything about his car and he was learning the series. I think he could have been a champion at whatever he wanted to do in the sport."

"In a very short time, Alan became one of our more respected drivers. No driver worked harder on his car. He was the heart and soul of his team." —KYLE PETTY

Born: December 14, 1954 (d. 1993)
Hometown: Greenfield, Wisconsin
The File: Celebrated each of his five NASCAR Winston Cup victories by circling the track in the wrong direction in his "Polish Victory Lap." Holder of a college degree in engineering, Kulwicki was an independent who was the most recent owner-driver to win the NASCAR Winston Cup title in 1992. Claimed championship by a margin of ten points over Bill Elliott in the closest NASCAR Winston Cup title race in history. Was NASCAR Winston Cup Rookie of the Year in 1986 and also raced ASA tour. Kulwicki led 20 races en route to 1992 championship, winning 2. Had 5 career wins plus 24 poles in 207 starts.

Like many of NASCAR's pioneer drivers, Tim Richmond had a larger-than-life persona.

Handsome. Witty. And very fast behind the wheel.

He quickly became a favorite with fans and media after jumping to the NASCAR Winston Cup Series a year after winning Rookie of the Year honors in the 1980 Indianapolis 500.

Richmond became one of the toughest drivers to beat on

Tim Richmond

NASCAR's road courses. Five of his thirteen victories and three of his fourteen poles in NASCAR's top division came on the road courses at Riverside, California, and Watkins Glen, New York. He won both races run at Riverside in 1982. In 1986, he won the Winston Western 500 from the pole at Riverside to complete his greatest season: third on points off seven race wins.

"Tim had that gift of being able to drive the car on the ragged edge and save it," said car owner Rick Hendrick. "I think the thing that impressed me most was his work on the road courses and at tracks like Charlotte, Darlington, and Pocono."

"You could put Tim Richmond in a covered wagon, and if it would steer to the left, he would get the most of it. No doubt in my mind, Tim was the closest thing out there to Dale Earnhardt." —CREW CHIEF LARRY MCREYNOLDS

Born: June 7, 1955 (d. 1989)
Hometown: Ashland, Ohio
The File: Richmond was a brilliant and versatile driver. Joined the NASCAR Winston Cup tour a year after winning Rookie of the Year at the 1980 Indianapolis 500. In 1986, led the season with 7 wins and finished a career-high third in the NASCAR Winston Cup point standings while driving for owner Rick Hendrick. Won 13 races and claimed 14 poles in 185 career NASCAR Winston Cup starts.

Darrell Waltrip

It almost seems to have been predestined.

About the time television fell in love with NASCAR Winston Cup racing, Darrell Waltrip was moving to the top of the win parade.

Flamboyant with an extremely quick wit, Waltrip was made for television. From the day he first crawled into a NASCAR Winston Cup car, Waltrip was outspoken which, at times, made him a controversial figure.

Waltrip never shied away from the cameras or confrontations. He raced hard and spoke his piece. He was successful, flashy, and a superb talker. For the media, Waltrip was a treasure chest. And he cherished his time in interviews. It was a love affair that couldn't have come at a better time for NASCAR Winston Cup racing.

As a result, Waltrip played a major role in helping NASCAR take full advantage of the new audience discovering it in the 1980s.

The timing was perfect.

On the track, Waltrip and car owner Junior Johnson dominated the early 1980s, winning forty races and three NASCAR Winston Cup titles in a five-year span.

That success put Waltrip in the spotlight. And the spotlight loved Darrell Waltrip.

"He gave stock car racing a face and a voice that the television cameras liked," said Junior Johnson. "When he won, it was a celebration."

Born: February 5, 1947
Hometown: Franklin, Tennessee
The File: The personable Waltrip ranks among NASCAR's all-time leaders in wins (tied for third with 84), starts, and poles. Won 3 NASCAR Winston Cup titles (1981, 1982, 1985) while driving for Junior Johnson. Twelve wins in both 1981 and 1982—the most since Richard Petty won 13 in 1975. Won 8 races from the pole in 1981 and had 21 top-three finishes in 31 starts. Forty-three of his wins and 34 poles came during six years with Johnson (1981–86). NASCAR's often-quoted elder statesman doubled as owner-driver for more than seven seasons beginning in 1991. Only five-time winner of Coca-Cola 600 at Charlotte. Won first Daytona 500 on seventeenth attempt in 1989.

"Darrell knew how to win on the track and sell off it, which became a very important combination for a driver." —ALAN KULWICKI

Former NASCAR Winston Cup champions Rusty Wallace (right) and Jeff Gordon battle side by side for the lead with Dale Jarrett in pursuit.

NASCAR approaches the millennium riding a wave of unprecedented popularity.

The 1990s have featured expansion on all fronts.

Three new tracks opened—California Speedway east of Los Angeles, Las Vegas Motor Speedway, and Texas Motor Speedway in Fort Worth—and one is being built in the greater Kansas City area.

And many existing tracks, including the original superspeedway, Darlington Raceway, were modernized and expanded.

It was a decade in which NASCAR ventured into the heart of open-wheel racing at the Indianapolis Motor Speedway and introduced Japan to American stock car racing. And NASCAR was a smash hit on both fronts.

"Tokyo is an important milestone not only for NASCAR, but for the U.S. Automobile industry," Bill France Jr. said during

NASCAR's first event at the Suzuka Circuitland in 1996. "Japan gives us a chance to present our sport to a worldwide audience."

The world was demanding more NASCAR racing. NASCAR expanded to meet the demand.

They added the NASCAR Craftsman Truck Series and expanded the schedule of both the NASCAR Winston Cup Series and the NASCAR Busch Series.

Attendance soared. Television ratings almost tripled. NASCAR became a family sport. More than a third of all fans are women.

As the horizons expanded, a new generation of drivers moved toward the front of the pack.

The leader was Jeff Gordon, who had two NASCAR Winston Cup Series championships to his credit before his

Future
Legends

twenty-seventh birthday. Compare that achievement to those of Richard Petty and Dale Earnhardt, who share the record with seven NASCAR Winston Cup titles. Petty was twenty-seven when he won his first NASCAR Winston Cup championship. Earnhardt was twenty-nine.

After five full seasons, Gordon had won nineteen of his career starts, a success rate that ranked him alongside NASCAR's all-time bests.

Gordon won a record $6,375,658 in 1997. He won ten races for a second straight year and his second title in three seasons. He already ranked fourth in career winnings.

But Gordon isn't alone.

The 1990s saw the emergence of the next generation of NASCAR champions. Again, the eras were melded together with Terry Labonte, Bill Elliott, Rusty Wallace, Ricky Rudd, and Geoff Bodine carrying forward the success they enjoyed during the 1980s. Other drivers like Dale Jarrett, Mark Martin, and Ernie Irvan really made their marks in the 1990s.

The line won't stop with the start of the twenty-first century, however.

The next wave of great drivers is already winning spots on NASCAR Winston Cup grids. And the greats after that are getting their starts on short tracks.

"It's really an amazing sport," Gordon said, reflecting on how his success paralleled a time of tremendous growth in NASCAR. "I know how all the drivers feel. It's just great being part of this."

No one knows what the future holds, only that there will be change.

Tracks continue to expand their existing facilities to meet ever-growing demand. Television coverage also continues to grow.

Even the manufacturers try new formulas. Although the Chevrolet Monte Carlos and Ford Thunderbirds were the backbone of NASCAR racing for more than a decade, both manufacturers tried other combinations. Chevy ran the Lumina in the late '80s and early '90s while Ford replaced the Thunderbird with the four-door Taurus in 1998. And Pontiac continues to make progress with its Grand Prix.

"These are exciting times for our sport," says Dale Earnhardt. "I'm proud of what we've accomplished. And the horizon looks brighter than ever."

Davey Allison was a superstar from the time of his first qualifying run for the 1987 Daytona 500. "An absolutely brilliant driver," said Neil Bonnett.

Of course, Allison had a legacy in the sport. He was the son of NASCAR legend Bobby Allison. Uncle Donnie was also a winner on the NASCAR Winston Cup circuit. And, as the youngest member of the famed Alabama Gang, Allison could also turn to Neil Bonnett and Red Farmer for support.

"I am here because this is where I belong," Allison said in 1988 of his decision to become a stock car racer. Days later, Allison would run second to his father in a memorable Daytona 500 finish.

"I gotta get one of these things, but today I am happy to run second to my dad," said Allison.

Four years later, Allison got his Daytona 500 victory. He was shooting to the top. He had won five NASCAR Winston Cup races in both 1991 and 1992 and finished third in points in both seasons.

"Davey Allison was a special talent: a great driver on the track, a quality person off the track," said car owner Robert Yates.

Davey Allison

"Davey was very aggressive . . . ran every lap like it was the last one."

—CREW CHIEF LARRY McREYNOLDS

Born: February 25, 1961 (d. 1993)
Hometown: Hueytown, Alabama
The File: Won 19 of 191 NASCAR Winston Cup starts including the 1992 Daytona 500. In 1987, became the first rookie ever to qualify for the front row of the Daytona 500. Won two races that year and was the NASCAR Winston Cup Rookie of the Year. A year later, ran second to his father in the Daytona 500. Won a career-best five races in both the 1991 and 1992 seasons and finished third in the final NASCAR Winston Cup points standings both times. Died in a helicopter crash on July 15, 1993.

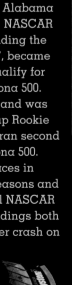

Bill Elliott

The nicknames flew as fast as Bill Elliott did in 1985. "Wild Bill." "Awesome Bill from Dawsonville." "Million-Dollar Bill."

And all fit.

Many experts believe that as much as the feats of Richard Petty and Dale Earnhardt, it was Elliott's amazing 1985 season that helped propel NASCAR Winston Cup racing to new heights.

Elliott won eleven poles and eleven races. Each of the wins was on a superspeedway, starting with the Daytona 500. He also won the Southern 500 at Darlington and the Winston 500 at Talladega to give him three of NASCAR's four crown jewels and the Winston Million bonus the first time it was offered.

And it wasn't just that he won. It was how he won. He won from the pole and he won from a lap down. He won tight duels, although he usually just ran away. The only thing he didn't win was the NASCAR Winston Cup title. Elliott finished second to Darrell Waltrip.

Elliott would again finish second in 1987 before claiming the NASCAR Winston Cup title in 1988—the first Ford driver to win since David Pearson in 1969.

Four years later, Elliott would finish second again, losing the title by ten points to Alan Kulwicki in the closest finish ever.

In 1995, he became an owner-driver with brother Ernie, again building the engines just as he had during that heady 1985 season.

"As far as I'm concerned, 'Bill Elliott' is just another way of saying fast."

—CAR OWNER HARRY MELLING

Born: October 8, 1955
Hometown: Dawsonville, Georgia
The File: The 1988 NASCAR Winston Cup champion is one of the most popular drivers in NASCAR history. Won his twelfth Most Popular Driver award in 1997 through the annual vote of the fans. Finished second in the NASCAR Winston Cup standings three times (1985, 1987, 1992). Named American Driver of the Year in 1985 and 1988. Won four straight races in 1992 to tie modern era record. Won the Daytona 500 en route to the Winston Million in 1985.

"Jeff is probably the
most talented driver to
come along in I don't
know how long. I've
never seen anyone
adapt to these cars as
fast as he did."

—TERRY LABONTE

Jeff Gordon

There is some truth to the rumor that Jeff Gordon was born to race.

He climbed behind the wheel of a go-kart at the age of three and began racing quarter-midgets at five.

But because California law prevented Gordon from racing professionally until he was sixteen, John Bickford, Gordon's stepfather, moved the family to Indiana to boost his driving career.

Gordon was campaigning midgets and sprint cars two years before he was old enough to hold a street license. At the age of eighteen, he became USAC's youngest national champion when he won the midget title. A year later, he won USAC's Silver Crown Series and was Rookie of the Year in the NASCAR Busch Series.

"Some of my earliest memories are watching races on television and copying what I saw," said Gordon. "And I used to play every video racing game I could find."

"As soon as Jeff started driving," said Bickford, "it was pretty clear that he had talent and a bunch of desire."

And quickly became a champion.

"He's not just the driver of the future," said Dale Jarrett. "He's the driver of the immediate future. Gordon's going to be a pain in our sides for a long time."

Born: August 4, 1971
Home: Pittsboro, Indiana
The File: The second youngest driver to ever win a NASCAR Winston Cup title. Gordon won 29 races and 2 NASCAR Winston Cup titles (1995 and 1997) in his first five full seasons. Finished second in 1996. Victories include the 1997 Daytona 500, the inaugural Brickyard 400 in 1994, three straight Southern 500s (1995–97), and the 1997 Winston Million. Made his NASCAR Winston Cup debut in the 1992 season finale that was also the last race of Richard Petty's career. Contracted by Rick Hendrick for 1993, Gordon made his debut by winning his 125-mile qualifying race for the Daytona 500. Won 27 races in first 94 starts for Hendrick.

Ernie Irvan

That Ernie Irvan lived to drive again was one of NASCAR's more heartwarming stories of the 1990s.

Just when it appeared that the rocket from California had found his place in the NASCAR Winston Cup Series, his world turned upside down.

Irvan was at the top of his game in 1994. He had three wins and ten top-three finishes in the season's first twenty races and was running second in the NASCAR Winston Cup points race, trailing seven-time champ Dale Earnhardt by a mere twenty points.

Irvan was putting on a show. Even though he missed the final eleven races, he finished the season as the tour's leader in laps led. He had also claimed five poles.

Then he suffered life-threatening injuries during a practice accident at Michigan Speedway on August 20. That night, Irvan was given a 10 percent chance of surviving.

Irvan capped a miraculous recovery by returning to action on October 1, 1995, at Martinsville Speedway. Despite wearing an eye patch because he was still suffering from double vision, Irvan finished sixth.

"All I focused on while I was recuperating was racing," said Irvan, who had won his first track championship back in California at the age of eighteen in a car built by him and his father.

Born: January 13, 1959
Hometown: Salinas, California
The File: One of the hardest active chargers in the NASCAR Winston Cup Series. Moved south from California in the early 1980s to pursue his dreams of a NASCAR Winston Cup career. Won 7 races, including the 1991 Daytona 500 while driving with the Morgan-McClure team. Finished fifth in 1991 NASCAR Winston Cup points standings. Had 3 wins and 10 top-three finishes in first 20 races of 1994 when injured in practice accident at Michigan Speedway. Returned to the cockpit the following year.

"Ernie runs as hard as anyone in the game."

—Car owner Robert Yates

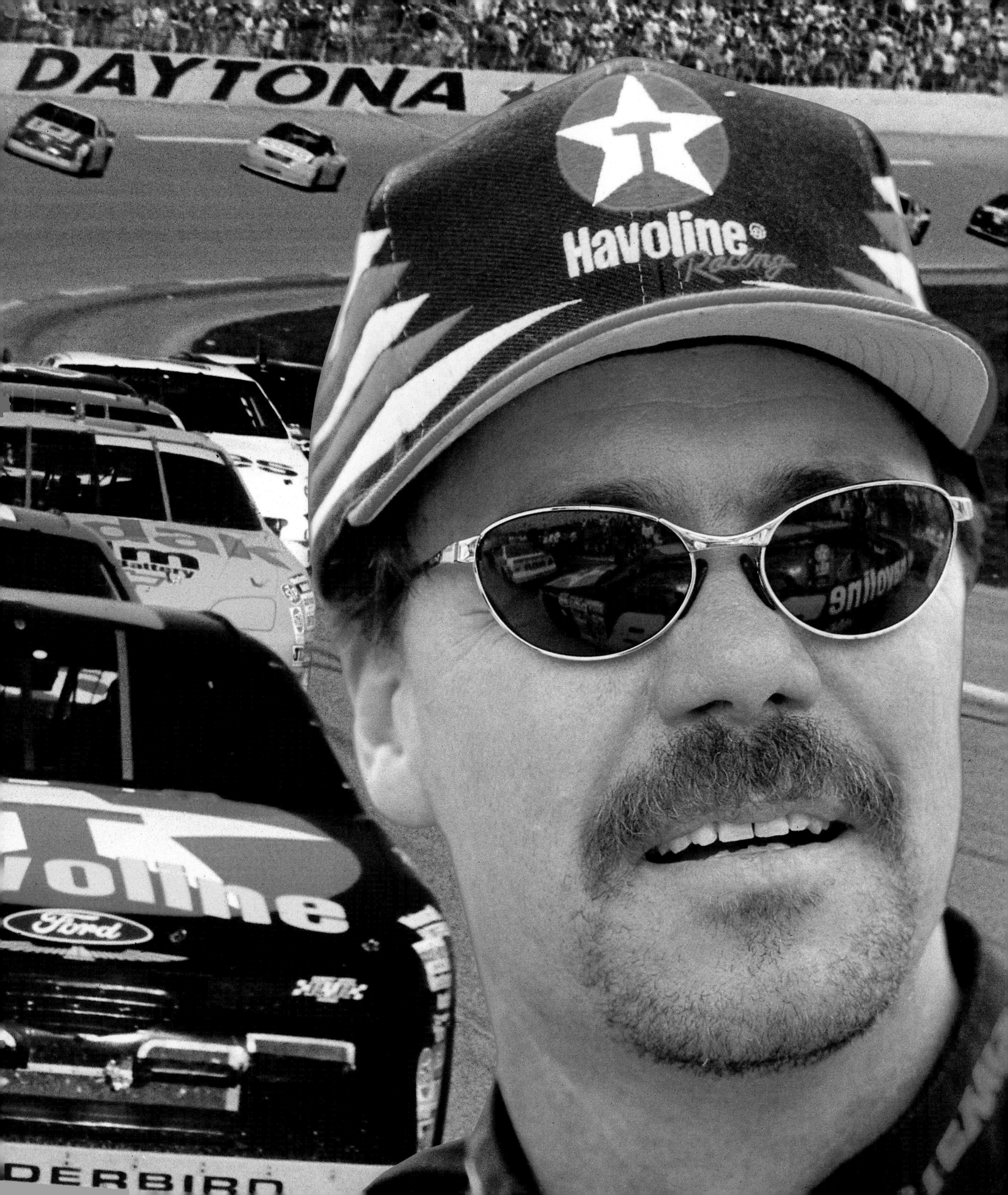
DAYTONA
Havoline
Racing
Ford
DERBIRD

If Dale Earnhardt is running fifth, he wants to be fourth. If he's fourth, he burns to be third. And if he's running second—watch out. Earnhardt—a.k.a. "the Intimidator"—might be the most "driven" driver ever to climb behind the wheel of a NASCAR Winston Cup car.

Winning is an absolute obsession. Yet, the man is also a genius at keeping a nonwinning car running in the top five.

Earnhardt is relentless and tenacious. But it is his touch of finesse that keeps damaged and noncompetitive equipment in the hunt.

During his six-championship association with car owner Richard Childress, Earnhardt has finished in the top three in 37 percent of the races he has started. He has failed to finish less than 7 percent of his starts.

He refuses to quit or back off—a lesson he learned from father Ralph Earnhardt, a two-time NASCAR Sportsman Division champion and another member of NASCAR's 50 Greatest Drivers.

"I grew up around cars and racing is all I ever wanted to do," said Earnhardt, whose son Dale Jr. is opening eyes in the NASCAR Busch Series.

Richard Petty will forever be NASCAR's King. But Earnhardt drives to the sport's soul. He is the classic, hard-nosed competitor who asks no quarter and gives none. He drives with a fire, which makes Earnhardt an icon to his partisan fans.

Dale Earnhardt

"There's Earnhardt and then there's everybody else. The biggest thing about Earnhardt is his desire," said car owner Bud Moore. "When he slides down into that race car, he is going to go to the front. If it's at all possible, he'll find a way to get there."

Born: April 29, 1951
Hometown: Kannapolis, North Carolina
The File: Won his seventh NASCAR Winston Cup title in 1994 to equal Richard Petty's record. Other wins came in 1980, 1986, 1987, 1990, 1991, and 1993. Considered one of the most talented and tenacious drivers in NASCAR history. Ranks sixth on the all-time NASCAR Winston Cup career win list. Only driver to go from Rookie of the Year (1979) to the Series champion (1980) in successive seasons. Career purses total more than $30 million. First Daytona 500 victory in 1998 followed 30 other wins at storied Daytona International Speedway. Five-time winner of National Motorsports Press Association's Driver of the Year award and two-time winner of American Driver of the Year honor (1987 and 1994).

"His desire and sheer determination to be the best at what he does is amazing. I've always thought he was the best, even when I raced against him."

—CAR OWNER RICHARD CHILDRESS

Born: November 26, 1956

Hometown: Hickory, North Carolina

The File: Son of Ned Jarrett, became one of the fastest rising stars in the NASCAR Winston Cup Series. Finished second in the final 1997 NASCAR Winston Cup standings, trailing champion Jeff Gordon by fourteen points in the second-closest finish ever. Won seven races, nearly equalling his previous career total of eight. Finished third in the final 1996 NASCAR Winston Cup standings and had four wins. Career took off after joining Robert Yates' team in 1995.

"It's very rare that you get a
driver who is fast and smooth
and still a perfectionist."
—CAR OWNER ROBERT YATES

Dale Jarrett

Dale Jarrett faced a decision coming out of high school.

Follow in the footsteps of his Hall of Fame father and pursue a career in NASCAR Winston Cup racing or try his hand at golf.

"At the time, I was a much better golfer than a driver," Jarrett joked.

He is still a scratch golfer. But Jarrett has developed into a great driver—joining his father as one of four father-son combinations among NASCAR's 50 Greatest Drivers.

But when Dale was facing his dilemma, father Ned, a two-time NASCAR Winston Cup champion— was leaning toward a golf career for his son.

"Racing can be a hard life," said Ned, who, before becoming a NASCAR television commentator, served as the track promoter at the Hickory, North Carolina, track where Dale got his start.

Only one major trophy eluded the senior Jarrett during his career. "I always wanted to win the Daytona 500 and I never did," he said. But he vicariously achieved that victory in 1993 as he made the call on national television as Dale sped to the checkered flag in the first of his two Daytona 500 victories.

Jarrett is the only driver to win NASCAR's two richest races— the Daytona 500 and the Brickyard 400 at Indianapolis—in the same season. He also won NASCAR's longest race, the Coca-Cola 600 at Charlotte, that same year to establish himself as one of NASCAR's top superspeedway drivers.

Depending on who you ask and when you ask them, Terry Labonte is either "the Iceman" or "the Ironman."

NASCAR's all-time leader in consecutive race starts is also one of the tour's calmer champions.

"I've learned a lot about how to race and how to be a professional being around Terry," said Jeff Gordon, Labonte's teammate on Rick Hendrick's team.

Labonte has quietly made his mark on the sport since he started racing quarter-midgets in his native Texas in 1964 at the age of seven. Although he finished fourth in his NASCAR Winston Cup debut (the Southern 500 of 1978), Labonte was considered a rookie in the talented 1979 class that included Dale Earnhardt and Harry Gant.

Labonte's forte is consistency. He has finished 54 percent of his starts in the top ten and has failed to finish less only 10 percent of his starts with Hendrick.

"The secret in NASCAR is tenacity," Labonte once said. "If things aren't going well, it would seem natural to suffer a letdown. But that's when you've got to race smarter than you would when you had a great car under you.

"I've always thought getting a third-place finish with a car that's not working right is just as rewarding as winning with a fast car."

"Terry has to be one of the coolest drivers NASCAR has ever had," said Dale Earnhardt. "Nothing bothers him."

Terry Labonte

Born: November 16, 1956
Hometown: Corpus Christi, Texas
The File: Two-time NASCAR Winston Cup champion. The twelve seasons between his championships (1984 and 1996) is a record. Those championship seasons were almost identical: Labonte had two wins and twenty-four top-ten finishes in both. Holds the record for consecutive NASCAR Winston Cup starts and has qualified for every NASCAR Winston Cup event since his rookie season of 1979. Finished fourth in NASCAR Winston Cup debut at Southern 500 in 1978 and won the race in 1980.

"I never knew all the qualities that Terry brought to the car until he joined our team. Great driver. Perfect team player."—CAR OWNER RICK HENDRICK

Mark Martin

The 1997 season offered proof of why Mark Martin is considered one of the most versatile drivers in NASCAR today.

He won six NASCAR Winston Cup races and finished third in the final points standings—coming closer to the title than any previous third-place finisher in NASCAR history.

He won six NASCAR Busch Series races to become the series all-time leader in career victories. And he won his second straight and record third title in the International Race of Champions.

Martin is equally at home on superspeedways, road courses, and short ovals. He is the only driver with three straight wins on the road course at Watkins Glen, New York, and is one of six drivers to win four straight races in NASCAR's modern era.

"I've always taken pride in meeting as many challenges as I could," said Martin, who is also a devoted body builder who follows a demanding training regimen.

"Each of us has only so much opportunity in our life," says Martin. "I just believe we should do everything we possibly can with the time we have."

For Martin that means racing a weekend doubleheader whenever possible.

"Mark's always right there near the lead no matter . . . Superspeedways, road courses, short tracks . . . Martin is good on all of them." —RUSTY WALLACE

Born: January 1, 1959
Hometown: Batesville, Arkansas
The File: Finished third in the NASCAR Winston Cup standings for the third time in 1997, but missed the title by only twenty-nine points. That was the closest a third-place finisher has ever come to the championship. Other third place finishes came in 1989 and 1993. Decade with car owner Jack Roush produced twenty-two victories and nine top-six finishes in the final NASCAR Winston Cup points standings. Also the all-time leader in NASCAR Busch Series victories.

Ricky Rudd grew up around cars—although not really great cars.

His father owned a salvage business and Ricky loved roaming the yard, going through cars and parts.

"That's really where I started to learn how cars were made and what works and what doesn't," said Rudd.

Rudd joined the NASCAR Winston Cup Series in 1975 and spent five of his first six seasons driving a family-owned car. Then he drove for some of the sport's top owners: Richard Childress, Bud Moore, and Rick Hendrick.

But Rudd always wanted to get back to owning and preparing what he drove and in 1994 became an owner-driver.

"Doing both is probably not for everyone," Rudd said. "But I found it's what got me really motivated again. I enjoy being involved in every aspect of racing: the managing, the car preparation, and the driving."

Rudd, whose highest finish in the final standings was second to Dale Earnhardt in 1991, placed fifth in his first season as an owner-driver in 1994 and sixth the following year. His victory in the 1997 Brickyard 400 was the nineteenth of his career and marked the fifteenth straight year that Rudd had won at least one race.

Born: September 12, 1956
Hometown: Chesapeake, Virginia
The File: Had won at least one race in fifteen straight seasons through the end of 1997. Ricky has been running as one of the more successful owner-drivers on the NASCAR Winston Cup Series since 1994. Has completed the most laps in a year three different times (1989, 1991, and 1994) during his NASCAR Winston Cup career. Entered 1998 with 19 wins and 23 poles.

Ricky Rudd

"Ricky was the most pleasant driver we ever worked with. He did a fine job for us. He knew what it took to win races, which is what I think has made him a successful owner-driver." —CAR OWNER BUD MOORE

Rusty Wallace

Born: August 14, 1956
Hometown: St. Louis, Missouri
The File: The 1989 NASCAR champion entered the 1998 season ranked third among active drivers in victories. Also placed second in the final 1988 and 1993 NASCAR Winston Cup standings. Finished in the top five 6 times. Considered one of the top road racers and short-track drivers among the present crop of drivers. Won races in 12 straight years. Paced the tour with 10 wins in 1993 and 8 in 1994.

"Rusty has all the ingredients you look for in a winner . . . smooth smart, and tenacious . . ."

—DALE EARNHARDT

It was only natural that Rusty Wallace and brothers Mike and Kenny became race car drivers.

Their father was a three-time track champion in Missouri.

"He gave me an appreciation of cars and racing," remembered Rusty. "I used to love going to the track. I'm another of these racers who grew up around cars and doing odd jobs for my dad.

"My two loves are racing and flying. And through racing, I've been able to do both."

Wallace's career has come full circle. He made his NASCAR Winston Cup debut for car owner Roger Penske in 1980, finishing second at Atlanta in his first start.

Although his only NASCAR Winston Cup title came while driving for former drag racer Raymond Beadle in 1989—a year after finishing second to Bill Elliott in the sixth-closest finish in history—more than half of Wallace's victories have come since rejoining Penske in 1991.

"Roger and I see racing the same way," said Wallace. "This is a profession and everything must be done to professional standards."

Professional is the perfect way to describe Rusty Wallace's two-decade NASCAR Winston Cup career.

"Rusty has taught me a lot about how you drive a race car," said Jeremy Mayfield. "There's a difference between driving a car and driving a race. And Rusty knows the difference."

Photography Credits

Daytona Racing Archives:
6, 9, 10, 11a-j, 13a-c, 14-15, 16a-b, 18-19, 19b, 20-21, 21b, 22a, 22-23, 24a-b, 25, 26a, 26-27, 28a-b, 29, 30, 31a-j, 33a-b, 34a, 34-35, 36a, 36-37, 38-39, 39b, 40a-b, 41a, 42-43, 43b, 44-45, 44b, 45b, 46-47, 47b, 48-49, 50, 51a-j, 53, 54-55, 55b, 56, 57, 58-59, 59b, 60-61, 60b, 62-63, 63b, 64a-b, 65, 66-67, 68a-b, 69a-b, 70, 71b-d, 71f-j, 80a, 84-85, 86, 87.

George Tiedemann:
2, 71e, 80b-d, 81, 82-83, 83b, 88a, 88b, 89, 90, 91f, 91h, 93a, 93b, 94a, 94b, 96a, 96b, 97, 100b, 101, 102b, 104b, 105, 106b, 107, 108b, 109, 110b.

International Speedway Corporation:
91d, 98b, 99, 102a, 104a, 106a, 108a, 110a.

Steve Baker:
71a, 77, 98a, 100a.

Kevin Halle:
1, 5.

Andre Alonso:
41b, 91j.

David Taylor/Allsport:
111.

Bill Hall:
85b.